Speaking the Truth in Love to Jehovah's Witnesses

Roland Cap Ehlke

NORTHWESTERN PUBLISHING HOUSE
Milwaukee, Wisconsin

Dedicated to

my longtime friend at

Northwestern Publishing House

Mark Sikorski

Library of Congress Control Number: 2007929764
Northwestern Publishing House
1250 N. 113th St., Milwaukee, WI 53226-3284
www.nph.net
© 2008 by Northwestern Publishing House
Published 2008
Printed in the United States of America
ISBN 978-0-8100-2059-7

Contents

Photographs

Illustrations

Introduction

Then we will no longer be infants, tossed back and forth by the waves, and blown here and there by every wind of teaching and by the cunning and craftiness of men in their deceitful scheming. Instead, speaking the truth in love, we will in all things grow up into him who is the Head, that is, Christ. (Ephesians 4:14,15)

It was a special day. The patriarch of a large family was celebrating his 90th birthday. Children, grandchildren, and other relatives had come from all over the state, and beyond. Tents had been set up on the spacious lawn, and caterers were serving a delicious chicken dinner. On the patio behind the house, musicians played songs from decades past, while people sang along. A warm midsummer sun heightened the festal feeling. Everything was just right, except . . .

The large cake especially ordered for the occasion had no words on its frosting. Among the many songs people sang, one was conspicuous by its absence. Unspoken, unwritten, and unsung were the words "Happy Birthday!"

The reason for this unusual celebration? Among the dozens of relatives—including this writer as a shirttail relation—were two people who do not believe in celebrating birthdays. In order not to offend them, the family had decided not to say the obvious—that this gathering was more than a family reunion. The persons being appeased are Jehovah's Witnesses.

Just who are these Witnesses? Often known as much for what they oppose—such as birthday and Christmas celebrations, saluting the flag, and giving blood—Jehovah's Witnesses remain a people outside mainstream society as well as outside mainstream religion. Our examination of the Jehovah's Witness faith will examine its history, what Witnesses believe, and how to share the gospel of Jesus Christ with them.

Much has been written and continues to come off the presses about the Jehovah's Witnesses. It is not the intent of this book to create experts who know everything about the movement. As shall be noted, Witness history is complex, and when it comes to the church's doctrine, its teaching, there has been a great deal of development and change.

More important than becoming specialists in everything Jehovah's Witnesses believe, we need to be firmly grounded in the Bible, which is the Word of God. We live in an age of religious indifference. Many churchgoing people are ill informed about their own faith, much less that of others. As we are more and more firmly established in our own faith, we will want to share it. Along with presenting Jehovah's Witness doctrine, we will present the counterpart in true scriptural teaching.

The Christian faith is unique. No other religion has the Savior, Jesus Christ. All other religions—and, as we shall see, that includes the Jehovah's Witnesses—teach some form of salvation through works. Although Jehovah's Witnesses have much to say about Jesus, they do not know him as the eternal Son of God and Savior. Many well-meaning Witnesses are devoting their lives to try to work their way into heaven. In biblical terms, they are trying to save themselves by their own righteousness, as they attempt to keep God's law.

Thousands upon thousands of Witnesses are giving their hearts and lives to their organization, which they believe is the one true church on earth. Yet Paul's words about his fellow Israelites also apply to the Jehovah's Witnesses: "I can testify about them that they are zealous for God, but their zeal is not based on knowledge. Since they did not know the righteousness that comes from God and sought to establish their own, they did not submit to God's righteousness. Christ is the end of the law so that there may be righteousness for everyone who believes" (Romans 10:2-4).

It is not the intent of this book merely to show that Jehovah's Witnesses are misguided. Rather, it is our hope and prayer that this small work will help many priceless souls come to faith in Jesus, who is the world's Savior. What a joy it is for Jehovah's Witnesses when they discover that Jesus Christ has done it all. He has lived for us, died for us, risen again, and promises us forgiveness and everlasting life. He is our righteousness and our salvation.

Research Notes

I have quoted rather extensively from Jehovah's Witness documents, believing readers should be able to examine and grapple with a sizeable sampling of the material for themselves, as well as through the filters of the author. Quoting from Jehovah's Witness sources can be difficult. For one thing, many of the older sources are difficult to find. Moreover, the organization has had a way of changing what it says from one edition of a book to the next, and it can be difficult to find the exact edition with the sought-after quotation.

Former Jehovah's Witness Duane Magnani has done researchers a priceless service; in his book *The Watchtower Files*, he not merely quotes from Witness sources, but he has reproduced entire pages photographically, so the reader can see the original document and the quotation in its context. When referring to this source, I reference the Jehovah's Witness source followed with the page in Magnani's work. The works of a number of other writers, in particular ex-Witness David A. Reed, contain yet more reproduced material from the Watchtower.

I am also greatly indebted to the many articles from the *Christian Research Journal* and to the Web site of Christian Apologetics and Research Ministry for the well-organized, concise, and complete information they offer on Jehovah's Witnesses, as well as other non-Christian religions and worldviews. The bibliography at the end of this book is extensive and includes many Jehovah's Witness sources, as well as numerous works by former Witnesses, who bring insiders' understanding to their critiques.

Above all, special thanks are due former Jehovah's Witnesses Don Luke and Amy Mueller, who share the Lutheran Christian faith with this writer. Amy and Don were kind enough to review the entire manuscript chapter by chapter as it was being written. In addition to offering personal insights and valuable suggestions, they added life and feeling to the material. They epitomize the Christian attitude the apostle Paul refers to as "speaking the truth in love."

Part 1.

The Nature of the Watchtower

1. Foundations of a Cult

North American society has become a spiritual supermarket, offering something for everyone—the careful shopper as well as the impulse buyer. That has not always been the case. At one point in our history, our religious tendencies were fairly homogeneous. That is, despite our denominational differences, we could all identify with a common religious core, something we referred to as our "Judeo-Christian tradition." Even folks who did not often attend church knew something about the religious consensus that constituted the "moral fabric" of our society. We were a Christian nation.

The religious scene is now very different . . . (Ronald Enroth, *New Religious Movements* 9)

Among the many movements offering their wares in today's religious supermarket is the Watchtower Society, better known as the Jehovah's Witnesses. In a number of areas, Jehovah's Witnesses hold traditional Christian values, and many people look at them as simply another Christian denomination. They believe in the Bible as God's inspired Word, although, as we shall see, they have their own adjusted version of the Bible. Witnesses stand for traditional family and sexual values, honoring marriage and the family unit, while rejecting abortion and homosexuality.

Nevertheless, like the Mormon church and other groups that deviate from biblical Christianity, Jehovah's Witnesses diverge widely from basic Christian beliefs. Although they make the claim that they represent the restoration of true Christianity and mark a return to the faith of our fathers, they are a non-Christian cult.

Common Characteristics of Cults

Relatively small groups, compared with major world religions

Follow a radical leader

Rigidly control members

Espouse extremist beliefs and practices

Reject historic Christianity, and place another authority above the Bible

Deny the Trinity

Deny the deity of Jesus

Emphasize salvation by work-righteousness

Tend to soften the teachings of sin and hell

Prey on the ignorance of nominal Christians and others

Feel a notch above orthodox Christians

The Nature of Cults

Within the Christian religion there are numerous denominations. Differences that divide the various church bodies are not to be taken lightly and can be highly charged. Baptists, for instance, reject infant Baptism, even though the rite is in keeping with the scriptural injunction to "make disciples of all nations, baptizing them . . ." without any distinction as to age (Matthew 28:19). While practicing infant Baptism, Roman Catholics, on the other hand, have added to the Bible the traditions and dogmas of their church, including that of the infallibility of the pope.

As serious as divisions between church bodies can be, the various groups are still considered Christian and are referred to by one another as denominations within Christianity. At times, newer and smaller splinter groups within Christendom are referred to as sects.

A cult, however, is something quite different. Cults differ not only in their dropping some teachings from the Bible or adding something to it, but they reject even the most central truths at the very heart of Christian faith. The two key doctrines that all Christians share are the Trinity and the incarnation of Jesus Christ. Both are mysteries, and both separate Christianity from all other worldviews and religions. The doctrine of the Trinity teaches that while there is only one true God, that God consists of three distinct persons—the Father, the Son, and the Holy Spirit. The incarnation is the truth that Jesus Christ is God in human flesh and blood (from the Latin, *in* + *carnis*, in the flesh).

Both doctrines are central to the truth that the second person of the triune God became a man, our brother, that he might live a perfect life on behalf of fallen, sinful humankind, and then offer that life as a sacrifice to pay for the sins of the world. Cults deny even these foundational doctrines.

It is ironic that the two major cults to come out of America—the Mormons and Jehovah's Witnesses—both claim to be Christian and to represent true Christianity. Their desire not to be referred to as cults comes in part from the fact that the term *cult* generally carries negative connotations. A recent book on the religions of the world offers this definition of *cult* in its glossary:

> A term used by sociologists to denote a nontradi-tional minority religion characteristically centered on a charismatic leader. Recently the term has been used negatively by the news media and others to designate a group perceived as making high demands on its members and controlling their lives in ways potentially dangerous to themselves and to society. (Ellwood and McGraw 514)

As far back as 1938, in *The Chaos of the Cult,* Jan Karel Van Baalen referred to cults as "the unpaid bills of the church" (12).

When churches do not do their God-given work, there is a price to pay in the form of new anti-Christian groups that challenge the most cherished and vital tenets of Christian faith.

Liberal Christian churches have failed in that they have caved in to the pressures of the times—whether in accepting scientific theories such as evolution over the biblical teaching of creation or in going along with social trends such as the acceptance of the homosexual lifestyle over against biblical morality. Other churches that hold more closely to the teachings of Scripture often turn people away by coming across as self-righteous, better-than-thou, and loveless. In either case, people turn to cults that offer something to believe in and a place where they can find a sense of personal worth and belonging.

The price people pay as members of cults is high. That price can come with financial demands made by their group, although for Jehovah's Witnesses, this is not the case. More significant, under the directives of a powerful leader or organization, people's thoughts and lives are strictly controlled. Instead of the gospel of full forgiveness and grace through Jesus Christ, cult members carry the heavy—and at times unbearable—burden of having to earn their salvation by following the demands of their organization. While they tend to look down on more traditional Christians as ignorant and unenlightened, cultists must close their minds to all but the dictates of their leadership.

In subsequent chapters we will examine the history, teachings, practices, and behaviors of Jehovah's Witnesses. The remainder of this chapter will discuss the place of the organization in the lives of Witnesses.

The Jehovah's Witness Organization

A key feature of the Jehovah's Witnesses is the strength of their organization. Witnesses know they are different and are proud of it. "There is a certain feeling one gets from being thought of as different," writes former Jehovah's Witness Ted

Dencher. "That feeling Jehovah's Witnesses have. They believe that God is restoring true worship to the earth and theirs is this worship" (24). Moreover, that heady sense of uniqueness—call it superiority—is heightened by a sense of being the only ones who will enjoy salvation. According to their official magazine, the *Watchtower,* only their church members will be saved (February 15, 1979, 30).

Dencher goes on to say how this sense of uniqueness impressed him when he was thinking of becoming a Jehovah's Witness. The conviction of Jehovah's Witnesses that they possess the truth and are members of the true church on earth is impressive—and heightened by their obvious devotion to their cause. Such dedication is especially impressive in our day, when many people believe there is no absolute truth and everything is relative. Whatever a person believes sincerely is thought to be true for that individual. In this respect, Witnesses come across as strongly committed to their truth.

Jehovah's Witness Terminology

In order to understand Jehovah's Witnesses, it helps to become familiar with a few key terms. The official name of the Jehovah's Witness organization is the Watchtower Bible and Tract Society (WBTS). Headquartered in Brooklyn, New York, the Watchtower Society prepares publications for the organization and oversees its operation.

Often the Watchtower is simply referred to by the all-encompassing designation "the organization." The organization of the Watchtower Society includes all the congregations of Jehovah's Witnesses, its leaders, its headquarters and branch offices, and its printing facilities. The organization lays claim to being God's sole organization and the only true religion on earth.

Along with its designation as "the organization," at times the Watchtower Bible and Tract Society is shortened to "the Society." As will become clear in our study, Witnesses must submit completely to the Society's authority.

Within the organization or Society, there are several special groups of people. One is the "anointed class." This is a group of 144,000 Witnesses chosen by God to rule in heaven with Jesus after they have died on earth. Jehovah's Witnesses believe that only this limited number of people will live in a spiritual heaven with King Jesus. All other faithful Jehovah's Witness believers will live in a paradise on earth.

The Governing Body is a central group within the organization. Its membership varies from approximately 11 to 17 anointed Witness men residing at the Watchtower headquarters in New York and claiming to be enlightened by Jehovah. For Witnesses, this group is the sole interpreter of the Bible, as well as the only channel of communication between God and all humankind. The Governing Body makes the rules all Witnesses are required to believe and obey.

The "great crowd" or "other sheep" consist of the multitude of people who are faithful to Jehovah but who have not been selected for heavenly life. They will live in the paradise established on earth after the great conflict of Armageddon, the battle that will bring the present order of things to an end.

The term *overseer* was formerly used in reference to an exemplary brother chosen by the Society to lead, supervise, and shepherd a congregation, in some ways similar to a pastor in a church. This arrangement was later replaced by a body of elders, yet the term is still used to describe the position of leadership over assemblies, conventions, circuits, districts, and branches.

For other Witness terminology, see the extensive vocabulary at the end of the book.

Set Apart

The Watchtower organization considers itself special and set apart from Christian churches, which in its eyes are not really Christian at all. Witnesses believe that for many centuries Christianity has been a corrupt, false religion—the great harlot,

11

Babylon the Great, of the book of Revelation. According to Jehovah's Witnesses, no sooner had the first generation of Christians—that of the apostles—died than a vast falling away from the true faith took place: "The death of the apostles removed a restraining influence, allowing a widespread apostasy to develop. (2 Thessalonians 2:7,8) An organization grew up that unworthily professed to be God's congregation. It falsely claimed to be the holy nation anointed with God's spirit to rule with Jesus" (*Watchtower,* June 15, 1992, 19).

From that early point on, until the coming of the Watchtower Society some 18 centuries later, Christendom lived in darkness. If this seems farfetched, that's because it is farfetched. As Christian writer Robert U. Finnerty comments:

> Perhaps the most compelling argument against a universal early apostasy may be found in the commissioning and empowering of the apostles themselves. If a universal apostasy occurred imme-diately after the death of the apostles, we would have to judge the apostles as incompetent or neg-ligent evangelists who utterly failed to accomplish Jesus' commission to make disciples. Such an apos-tasy would reflect poorly on Jehovah God as well, whose "holy spirit" was unable to preserve His followers for even a single generation. (18, 3:32)

Yet this is what Jehovah's Witnesses are asking people to believe. Witnesses consider historic, mainline Christian churches corrupt, decadent, and of the devil. Consequently, Witnesses do not view historic denominations—such as Lutherans—as fellow believers or even as misguided Christians. Former Jehovah's Witness David Reed explains:

> To a Jehovah's Witness, a church is just as foreign as a Hindu temple. In his mind a church is a demon-infested building surmounted by a pagan

symbol (the cross) . . . filled with immoral people
who worship a three-headed false god (the Trinity)
and salute an idol made of cloth (the national flag).
(quoted in Kern 9)

Given their conviction of having the only true church on
earth, Jehovah's Witnesses look down upon others, as ex-
Witness Joe Hewitt notes, "Ridicule of non-witnesses is an
integral part of the Watchtower society" (142).

That their organization is God's voice on earth is seen
especially in two titles by which they refer to it—Prophet and
Faithful and Discreet Slave.

The Organization as Prophet of God

The Society not only claims to be a voice for God, but *the
only* channel of God's truth (*Watchtower,* February 15, 1981,
19). The organization considers itself God's chosen prophet
on earth, as the *Watchtower* magazine states: "This 'prophet'
[referred to in Deuteronomy 18:14-22] was not one man, but
was a body of men and women. It was the small group of
footstep followers of Jesus Christ, known at that time as
International Bible Students. Today they are known as
Jehovah's Christian witnesses" (April 1, 1972, 197). Another
Watchtower article says, "Whom has God actually used as his
prophet? . . . Jehovah's Witnesses are deeply grateful today
that the plain facts show that God has been pleased to use
them" (January 15, 1959, 40-1).

The *Watchtower* magazine, which makes such pronouncements, is looked upon as God's communication with the
world. Back in 1939, the *Yearbook of Jehovah's Witnesses*
asserted, "It should be expected that the Lord would have a
means of communication to his people on the earth, and he has
clearly shown that the magazine called *Watchtower* is used for
that purpose" (85, reprinted in Magnani 15). Elsewhere, a
Watchtower official asserted that Jehovah God himself had
always been "the editor of the paper" (Magnani 16).

Cover of *Zion's Watch Tower*, Oct. 1, 1907

As God's prophet, the Watchtower organization considers itself theocratic—that is, ruled directly by God. The administrative system the Jehovah's Witnesses have developed supposedly rests upon that of the first Christians:

> The appointive powers rested in the hands of a governing body composed of the apostles and other mature associates such as Timothy and Titus. Similarly today the power of appointment of all servants rightfully rests with the governing body of the "faithful and discreet slave" class, which is under the direct supervision of Christ Jesus at the temple. (*Qualified to Be Ministers* 320)

The reference to "faithful and discreet slave" leads to the second key term by which Witnesses identify their organization.

The Organization as Faithful and Discreet Slave

In speaking of the end times, Jesus made reference to "the faithful and wise servant, whom the master has put in charge of the servants in his household" (Matthew 24:45). According to Jehovah's Witnesses, Christ was referring to their organization. At first, many felt that the organization's founder, Charles Taze Russell, was that faithful and wise servant (Magnani 25), a designation that Russell himself accepted.

> Thousands of the readers of Pastor Russell's writings believe that he filled the office of "that faithful and wise servant," and that his great work was giving to the Household of Faith meat in due season. His modesty and humility precluded him from openly claiming this title, but he admitted as much in private conversation. (*Watchtower* December 1, 1919, 357)

Today, the faithful and wise servant (or "discreet slave" in the Jehovah's Witness translation of the Bible) is generally seen as referring to the Society's leadership:

> Jesus foretold that among his people there would be a "faithful and discreet slave" class who would be providing the spiritual food to God's family . . . overseeing the carrying out of the Kingdom interests world wide. (Matt. 24:45-47). These anointed overseers serve as though being guided in their activities by the right hand of Christ. (*Watchtower*, January 15, 1969, 51)

Not only is the Watchtower organization perceived by its members as God's chosen prophet, but it is also his appointed overseer in the end times of the world.

Witnesses, then, see their organization as special, as chosen by God in these last times. That sense of uniqueness, sadly, is not based on Scripture. As will be evident in the course of our study, Jehovah's Witnesses have departed from even the most fundamental of biblical truths. They belong not to God's anointed organization, but to a non-Christian cult.

In closing this initial chapter, it is well to recognize the responsibility that Bible believing Christians have toward people caught up in cults. As Anthony Hoekema points out in *The Four Major Cults*:

> Cults have sometimes arisen because the established churches have failed to emphasize certain important aspects of religious life, or have neglected certain techniques. Though one may assign many reasons for the rapid growth of the cults, one reason we may be sure of: people often find in the cults emphases and practices which they miss in the established churches. (1)

This is not to say that individual Christians need bear a personal sense of guilt for the rise of the cults. Rather, it means we need to recognize that the churches have much to offer and should look for ways to improve in serving folks. We will want to give people everything we can for their spiritual well-being in response to the love of God in Jesus Christ.

2. Life in the Watchtower

The Watchtower leadership sensed that within Christendom were millions of professing Christians who were not well grounded in "the truths once delivered to the saints," and who would be rather easily pried loose from the churches and led into a new and revitalized Watchtower Organization. The Society calculated, and that rightly, that this would yield vast masses of men and women, if the whole matter were wisely attacked. (William Schnell, *Thirty Years a Watchtower Slave* 18)

A common characteristic of cults is their strict control over the beliefs and lives of members. Cult that it is, throughout its history, the Watchtower Society has had a tight hold on its members. This is necessary, for Witnesses see themselves as up against the kingdom of the devil himself, in particular in the form of organized Christian churches. As former

Witness Don Luke says, "Jehovah's Witnesses view all of Christendom as being led by Satan and under his control" (e-mail to author).

The Watchtower sees to it that its members are insulated from that world, well trained in what they believe, and disciplined in how they live. Then, having been properly prepared, Jehovah's Witnesses proceed to go out to win "vast masses of men and women" to their cause.

Sunday Morning at the Kingdom Hall

Jehovah's Witnesses spend two hours each Sunday morning in their Kingdom Hall; the first hour is devoted to the service and the second to Bible study. In some locations, several congregations may share the same Kingdom Hall, in which case, the gatherings will be in the morning for some congregations and in the afternoon for others.

The service meeting begins with an opening hymn from *Sing Praises to Jehovah,* which is followed by a prayer by an elder standing on the platform in front of the congregation. One of the brothers, perhaps from a neighboring congregation, offers a lengthy and well-prepared thematic talk on a subject such as sex and marriage, discipline, rebellion, science, or death. A closing hymn ends the session.

The Bible study follows immediately after the service, and most members stay for it. This is led by two elders on the platform, one who reads directly from the current issue of the *Watchtower* and the other who directs the reading and offers questions for members of the congregation to answer. Two ushers roam the aisles with microphones for people who raise their hands to offer answers. This session also ends with a hymn.

Watchtower Control Through Doctrine

At the local, congregational level, overseers watch the people and their behavior. Yet everyone in the organization is directed through the official publications of the Society, emanating from its New York center, known as Bethel. Such oversight and direction are so pervasive that the organization has been labeled Orwellian, after George Orwell's novel *1984*, which describes a futuristic society that is closely watched and directed by the leadership of "Big Brother" from above. The book *The Orwellian World of Jehovah's Witnesses* by erstwhile members of the group Heather and Gary Botting tackles this subject:

> Watch Tower Society publications give constant advice and counsel to Jehovah's Witnesses with a view to assisting them to achieve the goal of everlasting life in a future earthly paradise, promised as a reward for their obedience . . .
>
> Belief alone holds no promise of future life-everlasting, however. A strict code of conduct is imposed upon each individual by the society. (xxxii)

Of special influence is the semimonthly *Watchtower* magazine, from which we have already read several excerpts. The magazine's full title is *The Watchtower Announcing Jehovah's Kingdom*. First published in 1879, the *Watchtower* is the official theological publication of the Watchtower Bible and Tract Society.

As stated in the magazine's masthead, its purpose is "to exalt Jehovah God as Sovereign Lord of the universe. It [the *Watchtower*] keeps watch on world events as these fulfill Bible prophecy" (June 1, 2006, 2). The periodical's unsigned articles present the Society's positions on biblical doctrines. The following quotations from the *Watchtower*, arranged in chronological order, indicate how over the years the organization's stance on controlling its members, in particular regarding the study and understanding of the Bible, has been consistently strong:

> Theocratic ones will appreciate the Lord's visible organization and not be so foolish as to put against Jehovah's channel their own human reasoning and sentiment and personal feelings. (February 1, 1952, 79,80)

> Thus the Bible is an organizational book and belongs to the Christian congregation as an organization, not to individuals, regardless of how sincerely they may believe that they can interpret the Bible. (October 1, 1967, 587)

> We cannot claim to love God, yet deny his word and channel of communication. (October 1, 1967, 591)

> Only this organization functions for Jehovah's purpose and to his praise. To it alone God's Sacred Word, the Bible, is not a sealed book. (July 1, 1973, 402)

> We all need help to understand the Bible, and we cannot find the Scriptural guidance we need outside the "faithful and discreet slave" organization. (February 15, 1981)

> From time to time, there have arisen from among the ranks of Jehovah's people those, who, like the original Satan, have adopted an independent, faultfinding attitude . . . They say that it is sufficient to read the Bible exclusively, either alone or in small groups at home. But, strangely, through such "Bible reading," they have reverted right back to the apostate doctrines that commentaries by Christendom's clergy were teaching 100 years ago. (August 15, 1981)

> All who want to understand the Bible should appreciate that the "greatly diversified wisdom of God" can become known only through Jehovah's channel of communication, "the faithful and discreet slave." (October 1, 1994, 8)

Former Jehovah's Witness Joe Hewitt writes, "The Witnesses make heavy use of the words 'Bible study.' But in reality they study *The Watchtower* magazine and Watchtower books" (15). As Roman Catholics believe in the infallibility of the pope, so Jehovah's Witnesses believe in the infallibility of the Society, which is free to add and subtract doctrines, even as Catholicism has added teachings such as the Immaculate Conception (Hewitt 42).

In biblical Christianity, the church is built upon the rock of God's Word, the Bible. In the world of Jehovah's Witnesses, their organization is the rock that determines not only how the Bible is to be understood but even translated. Nevertheless, this is "rather cleverly masked," notes former Witness Amy Mueller (e-mail to author). Watchtower publications include numerous Bible references for Witnesses to look up and gain a scriptural knowledge that can be intimidating to outsiders.

Observing Sunday morning *Watchtower* studies in a Jehovah's Witness Kingdom Hall is eye opening. Everyone present is dressed up—men and boys in shirt and ties, women and girls in dresses. All listen attentively to two elders who stand on the platform in front of the congregation. One—off to the side—reads directly from the prescribed *Watchtower* article for that week. The other—at the lectern in the center of the platform—directs the proceedings with well-scripted introductions to the readings and periodic questions to the audience. Congregation members respond to the questions with pat answers from the *Watchtower* or by quoting appropriate Scripture passages from the *New World Translation* of the Bible. There is little spontaneity, and no one questions the official Watchtower view of Scripture. The Society has carefully trained its members to let the organization do their thinking for them.

Former high ranking Jehovah's Witness Raymond Franz points out the hypocrisy that such a system breeds, as over the years the organization would arbitrarily make contradictory decisions regarding its members in various parts of the world:

> I could not personally comprehend how grown men could fail to see inconsistency in all of this, could fail to be repelled by it, could not be deeply moved by its effect on people's lives. In the end it simply convinced me that "organizational loyalty" can lead people to incredible conclusions, allow them to rationalize away the grossest of inequities, relieve them from being particularly affected by any suffering their polices may cause. (135)

To question the Society in any way, above all in its teachings, meant that for such members "their relationship with God was subtly placed in question—along with their faith and wisdom. This is a form of intellectual intimidation" (Franz 163). After nearly 15 years, Don Luke's mother still tells him he needs to "return to the only true religion" (e-mail to author).

Organizational Discipline

The Watchtower Bible and Tract Society is a closed organization that stands apart from and in opposition to what it refers to as "this world." Members have their own world, which includes their own jargon. Former Witness Barbara Grizzuti Harrison notes, "Like any closed society, Witnesses have their own peculiar terminology. They talk to one another in a code that is impenetrable to outsiders" (23).

She goes on to describe the constantly changing nature of much of that terminology and gives an example of insider-speak: "In their publications, Jehovah's Witnesses use a lower-case *w* for witnesses: Jehovah's witnesses. To say *I am one of Jehovah's witnesses,* therefore, is to say not, I am a member of a strange cult with an esoteric name, but I am someone whom Jehovah has chosen to bear witness to His name" (24).

Language within the group becomes a way to control what the people think—and do. Yet language is not the main method of behavioral control. Chapter 10 of our study will examine specific areas in which the Society is widely known for exercising control over its people. At this point it is suffi-cient to discuss the driving motivation behind Jehovah's Witness behavior. While most Witnesses sincerely want to serve God, much of what compels them can be summed up in one word—*fear.*

That fear centers mainly in the thought of being disciplined and expelled from the organization. An Internet source, *Wikipedia,* neatly summarizes the steps involved in Jehovah's Witness discipline:

> Congregational discipline is administered by con-gregation elders through a judicial committee. In the event that an accusation is made concerning a baptized member and there is sufficient evidence, a tribunal or judicial committee (usually of three elders) is formed to administer spiritual help and correction. *Marking* is employed when someone who chooses a course that is ill-considered from a doctrinal standpoint, but still something for which the standard of disfellowshipping would not apply. Though such a person would not be shunned, social interaction outside of formal wor-ship settings would generally be discouraged. *Reproof* involves sins which are more serious than those for which one would be "marked." This reproof is administered before all who are aware of the possibly sinful issue.

During a two-week period, an announcement is made, mentioning by name the person and sin. The article goes on to explain the well-known practice of disfellowshiping (also commonly spelled with two *p*'s) by which members are removed form the organization:

> The most severe discipline administered is *disfellowshipping*. The standard put in place to determine if one should be disfellowshipped is the judgment of repentance. To judge repentance, members of the judicial committee ask detailed questions and review actions by the member being considered. . . . Baptized members who express disagreement on any doctrine can potentially be disfellowshipped for apostasy. Once the decision to disfellowship has been made, a person has seven days to appeal.

This process involves the asking of very detailed questions, with notes taken by the elders. If, for example, a person was drunk twice, that would provide two instances in which disfellowshiping may be in order. Indeed, the second instance can show a pattern and be interpreted as unrepentant wrongdoing. An appeal brings in three more elders to review the notes and ask additional questions. Very few appeals lead to the overturning of decisions, since, in Don Luke's words, Witnesses see Jehovah as "leading the elders correctly by his holy spirit" (e-mail to author).

The same process is followed when people leave on their own volition. They are told to sign a "letter of disassociation." When a person is disassociated or disfellowshiped, the announcement is made to the congregation that he or she "is no longer one of Jehovah's Witnesses" (Reed, *How to Rescue Your Loved One from the Watchtower* 19). Witnesses "shun" the individual, that is, cut off all association with him or her. They are not even to say hello if they meet on the street. Disfellowshiped family members living within the home are treated coldly; for those outside the home, there is little or no contact with their Jehovah's Witness relatives.

Being disfellowshiped carries heavy psychological and emotional consequences. For example, Amy Mueller relates how her parents had almost no contact with her because she had left the organization. Even after the passage of years, they refused to attend her wedding. To make matters "worse," she married a Lutheran pastor, thus joining herself with a leader of apostate Christendom. When she and her husband-to-be were engaged in the fall of 2001, her father responded to the news (coming shortly after September 11) by saying that marrying such a person was no different than marrying a Muslim like Osama bin Laden (e-mail to author). In Don Luke's case, he still cannot stay at his parents' house when in town.

Generally, fear of being disfellowshiped is strong enough to keep Witnesses from questioning the Society's pronouncements, even if they should involve change in teaching. As the spokesman for God, the organization has at times changed its doctrines or added new teachings, known as "new light." The organization likens such changes to a sailboat tacking in the wind; the doctrine may change, but the Society is still making progress. Even if such changes might disturb members, the fear of disfellowshiping has tended to keep them in line. Former Witness Hewitt writes, "What a disciplined Witness fears more than anything else is ostracism by his peers. To disagree with the Society on anything means being 'disfellowshipped,' being called an 'evil servant,' and losing one's eternal life. Therefore when the society comes out with *New Light,* every Witness accepts it" (20).

The Work of Witnessing

Driven by their devotion to the organization, Witnesses do what their name requires—they witness. Those who do such work are known as "publishers" or "Kingdom publishers." The typical publisher is a faithful part-time missionary (aver-

25

aging anywhere from 10 to 17 hours per month), who under the direction of the Watchtower Society shares Watchtower literature and doctrine with non-Witnesses door-to-door, participates in the Witness preaching activity, attends several weekly meetings and services (about five hours a week), and keeps records of missionary activities.

Those who do more than average work are called "pioneer publishers." While still doing the work on a voluntary basis, these Jehovah's Witnesses are in effect full-time ministers, whose field service is regularly 100 hours a month (more recently lowered to 90 hours a month). Even while serving as lay clergy, such workers manage to hold part-time jobs. Finally, there are the "special pioneers," full-time, salaried employees of the Watchtower Society, who spend 140 to 150 hours per month in religious service.

In their Kingdom Hall meetings, under the direction of the theocratic ministry school, Witnesses practice by role-playing. Then they go out to do the work. Witnesses go through the training and begin the actual work at an early age, for instance, age 6 (Mueller e-mail). Barbara Grizzuti Harrison recounts her experiences years ago as a door-to-door publisher in New York City, recalling (with a touch of humor) some of her opening statements:

> "Good morning. I have come to bring you good news about a perfect new world without crime . . .
>
> "I am bringing all your neighbors a message of comfort and hope from the Bible . . .
>
> "Hello. Isn't the weather beautiful today? Wouldn't you like to live in a world where the weather was always perfect? . . .
>
> "I've come with a message from the Lord." (I said that once, and a disembodied voice from behind a peephole said, "Tell the Lord to send it Western Union.")

26

Having made the appropriate introductions, the publishers do their witnessing. Each congregation has territories assigned to its area. A publisher checks out the territories and tracks that all households are contacted. Some houses might be noted as "Do Not Calls." Don Luke, who became a full-time pioneer in his early 20s, recalls one address with the note, "Man with a gun" (e-mail to author). Witnesses' work is not complete until they record the results of their labor. Grizzuti Harrison continues:

> Given any kind of opening, the Witnesses then recite a tidy little sermon, flipping their *New World Translation* of the Bible to well-worn passages; offer their literature; and depart—to record the reactions of the householder on a House-to-House record slip. They mark *I* for Interested; *NI* for Not Interested; *GW* for Goodwill; *O* for Opposed; *NH* for Not Home. These scrupulously kept records form the basis for return visits. (In 1956, the year I left the Witnesses—or, according to them, the year the Holy Spirit left me—it was estimated that each New York city block was "worked" by the Witnesses in this fashion three times a year.) (25-6)

Another former Witness, Ted Dencher, describes how he became caught up in door-to-door witnessing soon after being drawn into the organization:

> After I had been attending meetings regularly for a couple of months, a Witness friend suggested that I accompany him from door to door to see how the work is done. Having talked me into it, I agreed to go. There I saw that people *could* talk about the controversial subject of religion to total strangers and get away with it! Soon I was going house to house by myself. Gaining confidence, I began to pursue such activity every weekend. (15)

Not every publisher takes to the work with Hewitt's enthusiasm. Some admit that they never quite got over their nervousness or the rejection that is so much a part of door-to-door witnessing.

In order to prepare them for the experience, the Society tells its members that they can expect to be persecuted when they go out and share their teachings. "They are further told that this is simply the enemy fighting against God's organization because they are in 'the truth.' So, when someone disagrees with them, they are conditioned to reflect on what the Watchtower has told them. They then feel confirmed in being in God's true organization on earth (like all cults claim)" (Christian Apologetics and Research Ministry).

Into the Organization

Witnesses make bold claims in attempting to convert people to the religion. They assert that they have the only true Christian church, that they are God's true representatives, and that they have the only correct biblical teaching. Add the announcement that the kingdom of God is coming soon, and people's curiosity can be aroused. Former Witness David Reed warns, "It is usually much easier to free an individual from the Watchtower if his or her involvement can be nipped in the bud" (Reed, *How to Rescue Your Loved One* 21). Sadly, that is not always done.

Getting Hooked

While the vast majority of door-to-door visits yield few results for the organization, some bear fruit. Once an individual agrees to begin home "Bible studies" with the two pleasant Witnesses who come to the house, the web is being spun.

Within a few lessons, the churches of "Christendom" are discredited, as the prospect learns that Witnesses are the real Christians. Then the individual is taught that God must be referred to as Jehovah. After that comes indoctrination that "the dead go neither to heaven nor to hell but are unconscious and nonexistent" (Reed, *How to Rescue Your Loved One* 21). Christian churches need to step up the education of their members. Both Don and Amy note that Witnesses are better versed in Bible history than most Lutheran laypeople.

Step by step the convert is drawn into the Society— Jehovah's organization. Next comes baptism and the commitment to abide by the rules of the Watchtower. "Once someone becomes fully established as a new member, he or she typically enters a 'honeymoon' period during which it becomes almost impossible to penetrate his thinking. He has just made a public commitment and is surrounded by fellow Witnesses who shower him with love and attention" (Reed, *How to Rescue Your Loved One* 22). Eventually, the honeymoon will come to an end. But that can take a long time.

Growing Up as a Jehovah's Witness

While many come into the Watchtower Society as adults, some are lifelong members. What is it like to grow up as a Jehovah's Witness? Amy Mueller candidly shares some thoughts on growing up in the organization:

> I was born and raised a Jehovah's Witness. The maternal side of my family has been Jehovah's Witness for at least a generation. My father converted before he married my mother. My fraternal grandparents converted when I was about eight years old. Their background had originally been Roman Catholic.
>
> We were very orthodox in our worship and practices. We attended church three times weekly and went door-to-door every Saturday morning for three or four hours. My father, maternal grandfather and uncles were elders in various congregations.

29

There are no called or paid pastors in Jehovah's Witness congregations; the work of teaching, preaching, and shepherding is done by the body of elders. We did not celebrate any holidays or birthdays with the exception of wedding anniversaries.

There are no Jehovah's Witness schools; everyone attends public schools. When I was in school I was not allowed to join sports or teams that took up time after school. I was not usually allowed to socialize with my schoolmates outside of school unless an academic assignment was involved. Social activities were confined to those in the church. [Outsiders are known as "bad associations."] I was not allowed to date until I was out of high school. It was out of the question to date someone who was not a Jehovah's Witness. Dating, at least ten years ago, was also heavily chaperoned—even after an engagement.

It was highly discouraged to pursue higher education. It was stressed that devoting oneself to a career would take away from the ministry of God. Becoming a "pioneer" was highly encouraged of young single persons. Pioneers devoted 1,000 hours a year to door-to-door work. It was a sort of tent ministry idea—no church compensation was given.

It was a strict upbringing. On the other hand, my parents were loving, provided for all our needs, gave us appropriate discipline, instilled moral values, and taught us the importance of Bible study. (e-mail to author)

Eventually, she left the organization. Amy goes on to summarize that experience:

Even though my two younger sisters eventually left the church, I was probably the most difficult for my parents. Being disfellowshipped for immorality is not uncommon. Church members should shun you but it is understood that you will have contact with family members. I was considered an apostate because I left to join a different religion. This type of fellowshipping severs all ties.

Unlike some cults, Jehovah's Witnesses do not press their people for money. To the contrary, they are careful about asking for money. Donations are voluntary, and offerings are never taken during church services. Witnesses point out that Christendom is greedy and only interested in making the clergy wealthy and offerings in church services "shame" people into giving money. Nevertheless, the price for being a Jehovah's Witness is high. The life of a Jehovah's Witness centers in the Society and its demands.

Stressful as existence within the Society can be, for a Witness to leave his or her way of life is, to say the least, difficult. Elders, former Christians—including in some cases former clergy—and family members will pressure the person not to leave the organization.

A hymn entitled "Submitting to Theocratic Order" from the organization's songbook, *Sing Praises to Jehovah,* has an engaging melody and its opening stanza sums up the Witnesses' dedication to their cause:

> As Jehovah's people sound throughout the earth
> Truths about the Kingdom, of such priceless worth.
> Theocratic order they must all obey
> And remain united, loyalty display.
> *Chorus:*
> Loyal submission in recognition,
> This to our God we owe.
> He gives protection, tender affection.
> Loyalty to him we show.

3. History of the Society
(1): Beginnings

> . . . every indication of the Lord's providence has shown that God gave Brother Russell to the church to be as a mouthpiece for him; and those who claimed to have learned the truth apart from Brother Russell and his writings have been manifested by the Lord as deceivers, ready to lead the flock in their own way. (*The Watchtower,* September 15, 1922, 279)

To understand any religion, it is helpful to know something about its background, its roots. The Jehovah's Witness religion, officially known as the Watchtower and Tract Society, is relatively new, especially when we consider it within the broad panorama of world history. With its roots going back to the late 1800s, it is only a little more than a century old.

Unlike some other relatively new arrivals on the religious scene—such as the Baha'i faith, with its roots in Persia, or modern expressions of Hinduism, with their origins in ancient India—the Jehovah's Witness faith is not a foreign import. It originated in America. Yet in spite of being a non-Christian cult, as former Witness M. James Penton points out, the organization has its roots in "the religious environment of late 19th-century Protestantism" (14).

Key Dates in Early Jehovah's Witness History

1870 Charles Taze Russell begins Bible studies

1879 First issue of *Zion's Watch Tower and Herald of Christ's Presence*

1884 Zion's Watch Tower Tract Society incorporated

1914 Predicted year of Christ's return

1916 Russell dies

1917 Joseph Franklin Rutherford becomes second president of the Society

---

A Homegrown Religion

Nineteenth-century America experienced a great deal of upheaval that included momentous events such as the industrial revolution, westward expansion, and the Civil War. Partly in response to the turmoil that affected the lives of so many, that century saw a number of religious movements spring up, especially in the eastern part of the United States. Some of those groups are still thriving—Adventism, Mormonism, and Christian Science, along with Jehovah's Witnesses.

American religion was in a constant state of flux, with immigrants bringing their traditions from the Old World, while new sects sprang from the soil of the New World. Unlike the situation in Europe, American churches were not state churches and had to compete for members. The times and circumstances were ideal for self-styled preachers with little or no formal theological training to throw their hats into the ring and found their own churches. It was a time of religious revivals, marked by the so-called Second Great Awakening that was sparked by men like Charles G. Finney (1792–1875), the founder of modern, high-pressure revival preaching.

Out of this milieu came the Jehovah's Witness religion. As an American-born faith, the Watchtower Society is most similar to the Church of Jesus Christ of Latter-day Saints (the Mormons) and Christian Science, both of which go back to 19th-century eastern America.

In many ways the Jehovah's Witness church is a reflection of Mormonism. (For more background on Mormonism, refer to Mark J. Cares, *Speaking the Truth in Love to Mormons.* See the bibliography for publishing information.) Both have American origins. Both were started by dynamic self-styled religious leaders—the Mormons by Joseph Smith, the Witnesses by Charles Taze Russell. These founders were succeeded by equally powerful men, Brigham Young and Joseph Franklin Rutherford. Both groups claim to be Christian—indeed, the only expression of true Christianity in our age—when in reality they are cults which deny the very basics of Christianity. Both have been active in door-to-door witnessing and try to project a clean-cut, family-oriented image. Both have achieved worldwide influence.

In some ways, however, the Jehovah's Witness organization has had to play second fiddle to its counterpart. The Witnesses, officially known as the Watchtower and Tract Society, got off to a later start (1879 versus 1830). Although the Witnesses have enjoyed spectacular growth (with close to six million members in more than two hundred countries today), the Mormons are ahead (ten million members). Often the Mormons convey a more educated and cultured image— Brigham Young University, the Mormon Tabernacle Choir— than the Witnesses, who discourage higher education and whose membership has included popular musicians such as Michael Jackson and Prince.

Unlike the Mormons, who have added the *Book of Mormon* and other writings of Smith to the Bible, the Jehovah's Witnesses have added no new revelations to the Bible. Nevertheless, as will become evident, for all practical purposes, their "Bible studies" take the place of the Bible.

A brief review of the church's leadership is useful. Not only does it give us some insight into the people who have shaped the organization, but it will also help us understand how Watchtower doctrine and practice has developed through the years, at times changing dramatically with new leadership. The remainder of this chapter deals with the founder of the organization.

Charles Taze Russell, 1911

Charles Taze Russell

The founder of the Jehovah's Witnesses was Charles Taze Russell (1852–1916). Russell was a successful Pennsylvania men's clothing store owner whose deep interest in religious matters moved him to leave the world of business and found a new religion.

Russell was raised in a strict Presbyterian home, and his mother wanted him to become a minister. She said to him, "Charles, I want you to know that I gave you to the Lord as Samuel's mother gave him. It is my hope and prayer that in God's providence you may become a minister of the Gospel" (quoted in Botting 34). Russell shared his mother's dream, but he was repulsed by the church's teaching that God would condemn some people to suffer eternally in hell.

As a teenager, Russell rejected Presbyterianism for the more liberal Congregational church, which he also left. Explained Russell, "Gradually I was led to see that though each of the creeds contained some elements of truth, they were, on the whole, misleading and contradictory of God's Word" (quoted in *Jehovah's Witnesses: Proclaimers of God's Kingdom* 43). Much of Russell's subsequent career was devoted to denouncing organized religions as Babylon the Great, the great harlot of the book of Revelation (17:5; 18:2), one of several key components that would become a core of Jehovah's Witness doctrines.

Dissatisfied with the churches of his day, he became a religious seeker. He relates how, while walking near his store, "Seemingly by accident, one evening I dropped into a dusty, dingy hall, where I had heard religious services were held, to see if the handful who met there had anything more sensible to offer than the creeds of the great churches. There, for the first time, I heard something of the views of the Second Adventists . . ." (quoted in *Jehovah's Witnesses: Proclaimers* 43).

That experience, Russell declared, would "re-establish my wavering faith in the divine inspiration of the Bible" (quoted in *Jehovah's Witnesses: Proclaimers* 44). From that point on, he would be greatly influenced by the popular religious movement that has come to be known as Seventh Day Adventism. Influenced by the teachings of William Miller (1782–1849) and in large part founded by the "prophetess" Ellen G. White

(1827–1915), Adventists laid a great deal of emphasis on the end times and the return of Christ. Russell took up this emphasis, as well as the Adventist denial of the reality of hell. At the age of 18, Russell organized his own small Bible study group of which he eventually became "pastor," in spite of a lack of formal Bible training (Martin, *Kingdom of the Cults* 38).

In 1876, the same year he began publishing a series of books now known as *Studies in the Scriptures,* Russell met Nelson H. Barbour in Pittsburgh and adopted his eschatology (doctrine of the end times). Barbour had predicted the visible return of Christ in 1873 and, that failing, changed it to 1874. When that did not materialize, he and his group declared that Christ had returned in 1874 but invisibly. He would come for the end 40 years later, in 1914 (*Wikipedia* "Jehovah's Witnesses: History," June 11, 2006, 2-3).

The nature of Christ's return was a cause of division between the Russell-Barbour Adventists and other Adventists who expected a visible return of Christ. Wrote Russell, "We felt greatly grieved at the error of Second Adventists, who were expecting Christ in the flesh" (quoted in *Jehovah's Witnesses: Proclaimers* 45).

The two men broke from each other three years after they met because Barbour "denied the substitutionary value of Christ's death" (*Jehovah's Witnesses: Proclaimers* 47). Nevertheless, Russell retained most of Barbour's end-time views. Russell's penchant for setting end-time dates would become a hallmark of the Watchtower organization over the years. In 1891, for instance, he predicted that 1914 would mark "the full establishment of God in the earth." Later, the society explained that as an invisible return of Christ, even though the Bible says that "every eye will see him" when he returns (Revelation 1:7).

In 1879, Russell first published *Zion's Watch Tower and Herald of Christ's Presence,* forerunner of today's semimonthly magazine, *The Watchtower.* The early issues had a circulation of about 6,000 a month; today the magazine boasts a printing of 22 million each issue and is published in 137 languages worldwide. Breaking with the Adventists, Russell formed his own group, the International Bible Students Association.

On December 13, 1884, Russell incorporated "Zion's Watch Tower Tract Society" in Pittsburgh. This was the official beginning of the Jehovah's Witness movement. Members referred to themselves as "Bible Students," and outsiders called them "Russellites." Although the organization has long avoided using that name and plays down some of its connections with Russell, his influence lives on.

He wrote so extensively that the preface to his sermons claimed his writings on the Bible "are far more extensive than the combined writings of St. Paul, St. John, Arius, Waldo, Wycliffe, and Martin Luther—the six messengers of the church who preceded him" and "the place next to St. Paul in the gallery of fame as expounder of the Gospel of the Great Master will be occupied by Charles Taze Russell" (Clark 45-6). The year 1908 saw the transfer of the movement's headquarters to Brooklyn, New York, which would become the center of the Watchtower publishing empire.

Not only were Russell's writings voluminous, but he also claimed they were more important to read than the Bible itself! The September 15, 1910, *Watchtower* exclaimed concerning his *Studies in the Scriptures:*

> Furthermore, not only do we find that *people cannot see the divine plan in studying the Bible by itself,* but we see, also, that if anyone lays the SCRIPTURE STUDIES aside, even after he has used them, after he has become familiar with them, after he has read them for ten years—if he then lays them aside and ignores them and goes to the Bible alone, though he has understood his Bible for ten years, our experience shows that within two years *he goes into darkness.* On the

other hand, if he had merely read the SCRIPTURE STUDIES with their references, and had not read a page of the Bible, as such, he would be in the light at the end of two years, because he would have the light of the Scriptures. (quoted in Martin, *Kingdom of the Cults* 46, emphasis added)

Coming from anyone, much less a largely self-taught student of the Bible and self-made pastor, such claims are arrogant and cross over the edge into megalomania.

Russell did not hesitate to challenge centuries of Christian doctrine. Commenting on a remark Russell made that "the Lord has been pleased to use our humble talents," the official Watchtower history, *Jehovah's Witnesses: Proclaimers of God's Kingdom* states:

Russell thus was quite modest about his accomplishments. Nevertheless, the "scattered fragments of truth" that he brought together and presented to the Lord's people were free of the God-dishonoring pagan doctrines of the Trinity and immortality of the soul, which had become entrenched in the churches as a result of the great apostasy. Like no one at that time, Russell and his associates proclaimed worldwide the meaning of the Lord's return and of the divine purpose and what it involved. (49)

In spite of protestations to the contrary, Russell never was the Bible scholar he claimed to be. Under oath in court, for example, when confronted with his assertion that he read Greek (the original language of the New Testament), he had to admit that he could not read the Greek alphabet when a copy was placed before him (Martin, *Kingdom of the Cults* 43-4).

The point is not that only highly trained specialists are capable of understanding and expounding Scripture. Rather, it is that the Jehovah's Witness organization was founded by a man who was deceitful and whose insights into Scripture were largely borrowed from other errorists of his day.

Ever the entrepreneur, Russell began the building of a religious empire. He remained a successful businessman. Maintaining 99 percent ownership in his newly founded church, he still found time to become involved in scams such as the sale of "miracle wheat," which upon government inspection turned out to be "not five times as good as, but slightly inferior to, ordinary wheat" (Hoekema 226).

It is an odd coincidence that Russell, a would-be reformer, died on Reformation Day—October 31, 1916—while traveling on a transcontinental railroad through Waco, Texas, on one of his many trips to spread the word.

The grave marker of Charles Taze Russell in Pittsburgh identifies him as "the Laodicean Messenger"; Laodicea was the last mentioned of the seven churches of the book of Revelation (Revelation 3:14). Russell's followers consider him the seventh and last spokesman of the Christian church. During his long career he traveled more than a million miles, delivered more than 30,000 sermons, and wrote more than 50,000 pages (Hoekema 228).

What is more important, Russell's spiritual legacy lives on in his denial of the Trinity and the divinity of Jesus, which have remained mainstays of Watchtower theology, as has his assertion that organized religion, except his own, is satanic.

4. History of the Society
(2): From Rutherford On

Jehovah's Witnesses are a people widely known. Their preaching and way of worship have penetrated national and racial groups worldwide and have been embraced by people young and old, at every economic and educational level. Their zeal as Proclaimers of God's Kingdom has impressed even their critics. Their love toward one another makes some non-Witnesses wish that more people acted that way. (The Publishers, *Jehovah's Witnesses: Proclaimers of God's Kingdom* frontispiece)

As the above quotation from an official history declares, Jehovah's Witnesses are proud of their heritage and who they are. This chapter continues the history of the organization, showing its growth down to the present day. With the death of its founder, Charles Taze Russell, the Society's welfare came under the leadership of a dynamic successor, known to posterity as Judge Rutherford.

**Key Dates in Jehovah's Witness
History From Rutherford On**

1917   Joseph Franklin Rutherford becomes second president of the Society

1920s Door-to-door distribution of literature begins

1931   Organization named Jehovah's Witnesses

1942   Nathan H. Knorr becomes third president

1950   *New World Translation of the Holy Scriptures* issued

1975   Predicted year of Christ's return

1977   Frederick W. Franz becomes fourth president

1992   Milton G. Henschel becomes fifth president

2000   Don Adams becomes sixth president

Joseph Franklin Rutherford

Upon Russell's death, Joseph Franklin Rutherford—known as "Judge" Rutherford—took over the reins of the organization. Foreshadowing his later vocation in the Watchtower, to help pay his way through school, Rutherford had sold encyclopedias house to house. A skilled attorney and erstwhile judge from Missouri, Rutherford had served as legal counsel to help Russell through the entanglements of his controversial career.

If Russell had been a compelling leader, Rutherford was even more so. One history describes his appearance:

Joseph Franklin (Judge) Rutherford

The great personal magnetism and the air of mystery
which surround the man account most probably
for his success as a leader, for he was almost a
legendary figure even during his lifetime. The Judge
shunned photographs, although he was most
photogenic and presented both an imposing and
impressive figure when attired in his familiar
wing collar, bow tie and black suit. Reading
glasses, which hung on a string across his honor's
portly profile, accentuated the illusion of dignified
importance, along with the title of Judge . . .
(Martin, *Kingdom of the Cults* 48)

The transition of leadership was not smooth for the Judge
or for the Watchtower Society. Russell had instructed that the
organization's new president would share power with the

board of directors. On January 6, 1917, Rutherford was elected president of the Society, and at the same meeting new by-laws were passed that strengthened the president's authority. On the technicality that the board had omitted the formal re-election of its members at the annual meeting, Rutherford managed to unseat the majority of directors without calling a vote. At the same time, he called for a vote from the organization's local congregations, which further supported his position, while stirring up still more dissention (Hoekema 328-9; *Wikipedia,* "Jehovah's Witnesses: History," June 11, 2006, 3).

In the turmoil, a half dozen small groups broke off from the organization. A forceful individual and not shy to pronounce God's judgment, Rutherford declared they would suffer destruction for their actions. Yet splinter groups such as the Chicago Bible Students, Dawn Bible Students, and Laymen's Home Missionary Movement continue to this day. In 1918 the Pastoral Bible Institute was founded and began publishing *The Herald of Christ's Kingdom.*

Following in Russell's footsteps, the vituperative Rutherford became involved in legal entanglements, this time with the federal government. Watchtower opposition to mainline clergy support for World War I brought prosecution from the United States government. Along with his new board of directors, Rutherford was sentenced to 20 years in prison for violating the Espionage Act. Following the war, they were released on bail, charges were dropped, and the Judge emerged a martyr hero. The Watchtower history, *Jehovah's Witnesses: Proclaimers of God's Kingdom,* describes the jailed Witnesses as "victims of clergy-inspired persecution . . . like something out of the Inquisition" (70).

That same year, 1919, Rutherford introduced the magazine *The Golden Dawn,* now known as *Awake!* with circulation in the millions. Much of the Watchtower literature involved attacks on government, big business, Prohibition, the League of Nations, and the Roman Catholic Church. Regarding this last point, Rutherford personally challenged the pope to a debate, a challenge which, needless to say, was ignored.

Rutherford also taught that saluting the flag was wrong. In a 1935 radio sermon delivered in his deep, powerful voice, Rutherford gave his support to a young Witness who had refused to honor the flag:

> The refusal to salute the flag, and to stand mute, as this boy did, could injure no one. If one sincerely believes that God's commandment is against the saluting of flags, then to compel that person to salute a flag contrary to the word of God, and contrary to his conscience, works a great injury to that person. The State has no right by law or otherwise to work injury to the people. (*Jehovah's Witnesses: Proclaimers* 197)

In the United States, the refusal of Witnesses to knuckle under to government demands "drew mob violence against Witnesses as they preached and caused many Witness children to be expelled from public schools" (Answers.com, "Jehovah's Witnesses: History," July 3, 2006, 6).

Meanwhile, across the Atlantic, in Hitler's Nazi Germany, the refusal of Witnesses to go along with government demands led to thousands being sent to concentration camps. *Wikipedia* comments, "Members had the opportunity to escape persecution and personal harm by renouncing their religious beliefs. The courage the majority displayed in refusing to do so—in the face of torture, maltreatment in concentration camps, and sometimes execution—won them the respect of many contemporaries" ("History," June 21, 2006, 3). In chapter 10, we will return to the issue of not saluting the flag and other government-related matters.

Writing far more in less time than the prolific Russell, Rutherford wrote voluminously, more than a hundred books and pamphlets. Between 1921 and 1940, some 337 million copies of his books and materials were distributed (Gerstner 9). His writings include the book *Millions Now Living Will Never Die,* a volume that predicted end-time events for the year 1925, another subject we will return to (in chapter 8).

Like Russell, Rutherford left a lasting mark on the Watchtower organization. His bold rhetoric against established churches lives on; he would exclaim, for example, "Religion is a snare and a racket" (Answers.com, "History," July 3, 2006, 6). In 1931, he gave the organization the name Jehovah's Witnesses, based on the American Standard Version translation of Isaiah 43:12: "Ye are my witnesses, saith Jehovah." He was responsible for shifting the Society's emphasis from individual study to public witnessing work. By the late 1920s, door-to-door distribution of literature became a trait of Jehovah's Witnesses.

Under Rutherford, organization membership grew from 44,000 in 1928 to 115,000 in 1942 (*Wikipedia,* "History," June 21, 2006, 3). Moreover, during his tenure as president, the Watchtower Society shifted from a somewhat democratic organization, with local congregational involvement, to a more centralized "theocratic" organization run from its headquarters in Brooklyn (Hoekema 231).

Nathan H. Knorr

When Rutherford died in 1942, the Watchtower leadership passed to Nathan Homer Knorr. Lacking the flair of his predecessors, he focused members' attention on the organization rather than on himself. Known as an organization man, Knorr was a superb, if at times cold, administrator and oversaw the training of Witnesses. Previously they had carried portable phonographs from house to house and played recordings of Rutherford's speeches. Under Knorr's leadership, witnesses learned how to give presentations themselves. During Knorr's presidency, the organization grew from about 100,000 members to almost 5 million, the greatest growth it had ever seen.

Highlighting his career were the great conventions of Jehovah's Witnesses from all over the world. In 1958, some 250,000 Witnesses convened in New York City, filling Yankee Stadium, including the playing field, the nearby Polo Grounds, and outside overflow areas to hear the message "God's Kingdom Rules—Is the World's End Near?" At this gathering, 7,136 people were baptized into the religion, which, a Jehovah's Witness source reminds readers, was "well over twice the number that were baptized on the historic occasion of Pentecost" (*Jehovah's Witnesses: Proclaimers* 274).

During his presidency, the Society continued to pour out literature, every day producing enough books that if piled up could make a stack twice the height of the Empire State Building! ("Nathan Knorr's Armageddon"). Under Knorr, the Witnesses began the policy of publishing its materials anonymously. A look at the bibliography indicates that Witness books and tracts no longer bear authors' names. This was a major shift from the Russell and Rutherford days.

Most significant, the organization produced its own English translation of the Bible, the *New World Translation of the Holy Scriptures.* Witnesses consider this translation free from the "snare of religious traditionalism." Outsiders have criticized its misleading translations of key passages, especially those relating to the divinity of Jesus. The most noted of those is the *New World Translation*'s John 1:1: ". . . the Word was a god," instead of ". . . the Word was God." In subsequent chapters, we will examine specific passages from the *New World Translation.*

Along with huge membership gains under Knorr's administration, the organization expanded greatly throughout the world. When he took over in 1942, the Society was active in 54 countries; by 1961 that had expanded to 185 countries (Hoekema 233). During the Knorr era, Watchtower power became less centralized once again; the board was expanded from 7 to 11 members; with the president making the number

12, reminiscent of the Twelve disciples. Though the organization was less centralized, Knorr still retained much of the organization's power. His successor, however, would inherit a less influential presidency.

Fredrick W. Franz

In 1977 Frederick W. Franz became the Society's fourth president. He joined the church under Russell and had been working at the Brooklyn headquarters since 1920. During the Knorr years, he was the leading theologian and anonymous writer behind Watchtower publications. He is generally recognized as the main translator of the *New World Translation.*

As was the case with his predecessor, under Franz' leadership, the organization continued to pour out a flood of anonymous publications. Yet Franz stepped into the leadership of a troubled organization. Prior to his presidency, he had been instrumental in developing church doctrine, including the prediction of 1975 as the year the world would end. The failure of that prophecy left many members discontented. Many left the Society. (Chapter 8 will take up the topic of Jehovah's Witness end-time prophecies.)

After decades of rapid growth, the church began losing members. Together with other leaders, Franz broke up independent Bible study groups and set up committees to try members who were disloyal. His own nephew and member of the governing board, Raymond V. Franz, was forced to resign.

The legacy of Fredrick Franz was mainly theological. For 50 years—from the beginning of Knorr's presidency until 1992—Franz was the church's leading theologian. He was adamant about Watchtower control over members' study of Scripture. On one occasion, when speaking to a Spanish congregation in New York, "Franz himself shouted at the congregation in heavily accented Spanish to insist that Bible study be carried on at the kingdom hall and not in the privacy of their homes" (Penton 121).

Fredrick Franz symbolized the aging, first generation of Watchtower membership, which believed that it would live to see the return of Christ. He died in 1992 at the age of 99, leaving behind a Governing Body mostly in their 80s and 90s. Until Franz' passing, then, for more than a century, only four men had led the Watchtower organization.

Milton G. Henschel

Franz' successor was Milton G. Henschel, who was 72 at the time he assumed the presidency on December 30, 1992. As second youngest of the Watchtower's governing board, Henschel was part of the old guard that was rapidly passing from the scene.

Much of previous Watchtower teaching and practice revolved around the generation that was alive during the early years. According to Jehovah's Witness doctrine, only men who had been baptized into the organization during or before 1935 could lead it. In that year, the number of 144,000 had been reached; these were considered part of the "body of Christ," the "anointed" or "heavenly" class, who would inherit heaven. Judge Rutherford had proclaimed that any to come into the organization after that would be among the "great crowd," those destined not to enter heaven but to live in a paradise on earth.

In October 2000, Henschel resigned as president and was replaced by a younger man, Don Adams. (Henschel died in 2003.) Henschel's resignation marked part of a major reorganization of the Society. While Henschel had stepped down as president, he remained a member of the Governing Body, a group of older spiritual leaders, which up to that point had been identical with the corporation's board of directors.

This change in leadership helped protect the Society from potential lawsuits, resulting for instance from its ban on blood transfusions (see chapter 10). People cannot sue the corporation, which is now separate from the moral leadership of the Governing Body.

A Changing Organization

The Watchtower needed to develop new teachings to accommodate the passing of the old generation. We will discuss this in more detail as we get into specific teachings, but the following quote from M. Kurt Goeldelman helps put the Watchtower situation in perspective:

> According to Watchtower teaching, "anointed" Christians are a select body of 144,000 persons consisting of believers from the first century up until the present day. Jehovah's Witnesses maintain the total number of this group, which is interpreted from Revelation 7:14, was fulfilled in the 1930s. According to the Society's figures, fewer than 9,000 of the elite are presently [2001] alive on the earth. Most members of this remnant are aged and the shrinking number posed challenges in selecting Watchtower officers under its previous criterion. (1)

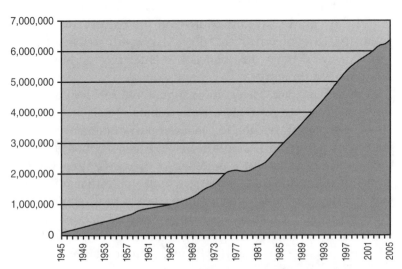

Line chart of Jehovah's Witness membership 1945–2005

Along the same lines, in "Whither the Watchtower?: An Unfolding Crisis for Jehovah's Witnesses," David Reed points out that according to the organization's teachings, Christ returned invisibly in 1914 and "selected Watchtower leaders to rule the earthly realm of his kingdom." That generation of leaders has all but died off.

Not only does the Watchtower face the passing of its founding generations, but it also faces other challenges as well. In the past, the Jehovah's Witnesses have adjusted to problems and changed. As a matter of fact, change has been an integral part of the organization's history, as evidenced in some of the adjustments during transitions in leadership.

As we will see, changes have involved much more than organizational issues or practices. The Watchtower has a long-standing history of doctrinal change. This has been especially true in topics relating to the time of Christ's return (chapter 8), but other issues are involved as well.

More than that, the Jehovah's Witnesses have drawn on various sources for their doctrines, beginning with the connection to Adventist teachings about the imminent return of Jesus. Beliefs concerning the end of time have changed with the passing of years and with the failed fulfillment of Witness prophecies. The Watchtower view of Jesus resurrects an ancient church heresy (chapter 4 and appendix). Other Watchtower beliefs have been shaped and reshaped as the church's history has developed. The church's position on whether or not to worship Jesus is an example of this. As we discuss specific teachings of the church in subsequent chapters, we will take note of such doctrinal changes.

Today church membership numbers close to six million, with five out of six members living outside the United States. (For fairly recent statistics on the organization, see *Wikipedia* online.) There is a great influx of new members into the Watchtower, but that is offset by a large turnover rate. Yet it is unwise to think that the organization is about to fold. It has faced crises before and come out even stronger. Especially known for its publications, the organization has developed a huge publishing empire. Some of the many publications are available in as many as 410 languages (*Wikipedia,* "Jehovah's Witnesses: Beliefs and Practices," June 21, 2006, 6).

For Christians, of course, it is important to look at Jehovah's Witnesses not as statistics but as priceless blood-bought souls. Jesus Christ died for them, as he did for the whole world. Our goal is to share the good news of salvation with all.

Outside of the Society's official account, Jehovah's Witnesses are discouraged from looking into their history or old Watchtower literature, which is filled with contradictions, doctrinal changes, and false prophecies (see chapter 8). Instead, they are indoctrinated against the basic Christian teachings of the Trinity and the divinity of Jesus Christ. This is the subject of the next section of our study.

Part 2.
The Watchtower
and the Bible

5. The Bible and
the Nature of God

If you ask a clergyman what is meant by the trinity he says: "That is a mystery." He does not know, and no one else knows, because it is false.

Never was there a more deceptive doctrine advanced than that of the trinity. It could have originated only in one mind, and that the mind of Satan the Devil.

The purpose was and is to produce confusion in the mind of man and to destroy the true philosophy of the great ransom sacrifice. (Jehovah's Witness 1928 publication *Reconciliation* 101)

Many churchgoers have little or no knowledge of the belief systems of other religions, including that of Jehovah's Witnesses. "People need to know how different their teachings are," states Don Luke. "Most people I talk to have no idea, but think they [Jehovah's Witnesses] are just good people." Using their own translation of the Bible and eclectically enlisting scattered sources to bolster their contentions, they reject the most fundamental Christian teachings, including that of the Trinity.

Key Passages on the Scriptures and God

The Scriptures:

"All Scripture is God-breathed and is useful for teaching, rebuking, correcting and training in righteousness" (2 Timothy 3:16).

The Nature of God:

"Hear, O Israel: The Lord our God, the Lord is one" (Deuteronomy 6:4).

Jesus said, "Therefore go and make disciples of all nations, baptizing them in the name of the Father and of the Son and of the Holy Spirit" (Matthew 28:19).

The Source of Faith

For Christians, the foundation of their faith is the Word of God—the 66 books of the Bible. As Paul says, "All Scripture is God-breathed" (2 Timothy 3:16). That means the Bible is inspired and as such is inerrant and authoritative. Witnesses also speak of the inspiration, truthfulness, and authority of the Bible (*Aid to Bible Understanding* 228-32). But with a twist.

At least in theory, Jehovah's Witnesses follow the principle of *sola scriptura*—Scripture alone—as espoused by Martin Luther and other reformers, who opposed the notion that only the Roman Catholic Church could interpret the Bible. The Witness book *Let God Be True* declares, "To let God be true means to let God have the say as to what is the truth that makes men free. It means to accept his Word, the Bible, as the truth. . . . Our obligation is to back up what is said herein by quotations from the Bible for proof of truthfulness and reliability" (9-10).

Elsewhere, in defining who they are, Witnesses emphasize their reliance on the Bible alone: "Jehovah's Witnesses Definition: The worldwide Christian society of people who actively bear witness regarding Jehovah God and his purposes affecting mankind. They base their beliefs solely on the Bible" (*Reasoning from the Scriptures* 199).

In order to ensure the integrity of the Bible it uses, the Watchtower has its own translation, the *New World Translation of the Holy Scriptures.* Witnesses believe that the *New World Translation* is the true and accurate translation, while others are distorted by the bias of the translators. As one reads more in this translation and in Jehovah's Witness commentaries and Bible studies related to it, a pattern becomes clear. This translation is not the work of learned scholars—only Fredrick Franz had any training in Greek, the original language of the New Testament, and he was self-taught in Hebrew, the language of the Old. When challenged under oath, Franz had to admit that he was far from a first-rate Hebrew scholar (Martin, *Kingdom of the Cults* 72-3). Rather than drawing upon the meaning of the original text of Scriptures, the Watchtower translators fit the translation to their doctrine.

In addition to having their own Bible, Witnesses consider their Bible study materials to be the only sure guides to understanding God's Word. In a statement we have already noted, the *Watchtower* claims that the organization must interpret Scripture for the people, "Thus the Bible is an organizational book and belongs to the Christian congregation as an organization, not to individuals, regardless of how sincerely they may believe that they can interpret the Bible" (October 1, 1967, 587).

Having developed their own translation, they have scoured through various Christian writings to find comments that would agree with their rendering of the text and bolster the points they make in their publications. The use of these sources gives an impression of scholarship, but it is an illusion.

The real source of Watchtower belief is not God's revelation in Scripture but the conclusions of human reason, as expounded by the organization's Governing Body. This reliance on reason goes back to Charles Taze Russell, who rejected the doctrine of hell and the Trinity as unreasonable. (See chapter 5, "The Foundation of Jehovah's Witness Beliefs," in Bowman, *Understanding Jehovah's Witnesses* 75-84.) According to Jehovah's Witnesses, "Reasonableness is a distinctive feature of heavenly wisdom" (*Aid to Bible Understanding* 1376).

Time and again, Witnesses will attack what seems unreasonable. They reject the very idea of hell, arguing that it is unreasonable for a loving God to inflict such a punishment on people. Moreover, they join every non-Christian religion or philosophy in discrediting the two key mysteries of Scripture—the Trinity and the incarnation of Jesus Christ—both of which cannot be grasped by human reason. Instead, they offer up their version of God, who, they insist, must be called by the name Jehovah.

The Name of God

Throughout the Bible, God's name is whatever he has disclosed or revealed about himself. He is known by many different names.

In the Old Testament there are two particular names by which God has made himself known. One is the word *God,* which in Hebrew, the original language of the Old Testament, is *Elohim.* This word is of interest for several reasons, including its use in many names, such as Bethel, "House of God." Moreover, even though it usually refers to the one true God, it is actually a plural (the Hebrew masculine plural ending *–im*). So the very word *God* carries with it the idea of plurality.

The other most common term is LORD, often rendered in translations with all capital letters to distinguish it from just any lord. The background behind this word is also fascinating. The written Hebrew language was consonantal; that is, the consonants were written, but the vowels had to be supplied by the reader. To make somewhat of an analogy, if this were the case in English, the consonants *ct* might be read as *cat, cot,* or *cut,* with the context supplying the reader with an awareness of which one fits.

The consonant letters for the name LORD in Hebrew are often depicted on symbols or logos and are known as the Tetragrammaton (the Four Letters); they look like this: יהוה (the Hebrew script reads from right to left). The word can be transcribed in English as YHWH or possibly JHVH. Whenever the ancient Jews came to that name, however, they refrained from pronouncing it, considering it too sacred to be spoken. Instead, they would say the Hebrew word *Adonai,* that is, Lord (hence the translation LORD). Later, people decided that the name would be pronounced Yahweh or, less likely, Jehovah. The latter form of the word is the one that Jehovah's Witnesses have taken up.

There is more behind this special name. The name of the LORD traces back to Exodus chapter 3, where God explained the name to Moses. This is a point we will take up in our discussion of the divinity of Jesus.

Jehovah's Witnesses insist that Jehovah "is the only proper name for God" (Kern 8). In answer to the question, "Why is it important to know and use God's personal name?" the Jehovah's Witness book *Reasoning from the Scriptures* states:

> Do you have a close relationship with anyone whose personal name you do not know? For people to whom God is nameless he is often merely an impersonal force, not a real person, not someone that they know and love and to whom they can speak from the heart in prayer. If they do pray, their prayers are merely a ritual, a formalistic repetition of memorized expressions.
>
> True Christians have a commission from Jesus Christ to make disciples of people of all nations. When teaching these people, how would it be possible to identify the true God as different from the false gods of the nations? Only by using His personal name, as the Bible itself does.—Matt. 28:19,20; 1 Cor. 8:5,6.
>
> Ex. 3:15: "God said. . . to Moses: 'This is what you are to say to the sons of Israel, "Jehovah the God of your forefathers . . . has sent me to you." This is my name to time indefinite, and this is the memorial of me to generation after generation.'"
>
> Isa. 12:4: "Give thanks to Jehovah, you people! Call upon his name. Make known among the peoples his dealings. Make mention that his name is put on high." (196-7)

The listing of passages goes on. This excerpt illustrates the typical Witness use of scriptural passages to bolster an argument they are setting forth. Having insisted on the use of the name Jehovah, they list numerous passages from the *New World Translation* that use the word.

Despite Witness protestations to the contrary—and finding the rare scholar who might happen to agree with them in some particular point—the word *Jehovah* is "an artificial form," going back perhaps to about A.D. 1520 (Kern 39). Yet they contend its use is the very hallmark of true religion (*You Can Live Forever in Paradise on Earth* 184-5). *The New World Translation* goes so far as to insert Jehovah in the New Testament 237 times, even though the word is not there, and Jesus never referred to God as Jehovah (Reed, *Jehovah's Witnesses Answered Verse by Verse* 18).

Romans 14:8,9 furnishes an example of this; the *New World Translation* states: ". . . if we live, we live to Jehovah and if we die, we die to Jehovah. Therefore both if we live and if we die, we belong to Jehovah. For to this end Christ died and came to life again, that he might be Lord over both the dead and the living." The Greek root translated three times as "Jehovah" is *kyrios,* the same Greek word translated as "Lord" when referring to Christ. When the word clearly refers to God, they translate it Jehovah, but when it (as a verb form, "be Lord") refers to Christ, they refuse to translate it the same way, even when it occurs in the same context. They refuse to recognize that Jesus is Jehovah.

The Biblical Doctrine of the Trinity

While insisting on the use of the word *Jehovah,* the Society rejects the entire concept of the Trinity, since that word is not found in Scripture. Granted, the Bible does not use the words *Trinity* or *triune*. Nevertheless, it clearly teaches that God is three (tri) distinct divine persons in one (-une) God. Scripture states, "Hear, O Israel: The LORD our God, the LORD is one" (Deuteronomy 6:4), a passage Jesus quotes approvingly (Mark 12:29).

Elsewhere, Scripture speaks more explicitly of a plurality within the Godhead. Already in Genesis chapter 1, when God created the heavens and the earth, "the Spirit of God was hovering over the waters" (1:2), indicating the presence of the Holy Spirit. As noted, the Hebrew word for God, *Elohim*, is a plural, even though it uses a singular verb. Thus God says,

"Let us make man in our image, in our likeness" (1:26). This is not merely a "majestic plural," for the Old Testament often alludes to a plurality within the deity.

That plurality is present in other passages, as when Abraham was about to sacrifice Isaac, the Bible says, "[T]he angel of the Lord called out to him from heaven . . . 'Do not lay a hand on the boy. . . . Now I know that you fear *God*, because you have not withheld from *me* your son'" (Genesis 22:11,12, italics added). Here and elsewhere this special angel (messenger) of the Lord both speaks on behalf of God *and* as God.

These same three persons appear in the New Testament: God the Father, the Son (the Word), and the Holy Spirit. Jesus brings it all together when he says, "All authority in heaven and on earth has been given to me. Therefore go and make disciples of all nations, baptizing them in the name of the Father and of the Son and of the Holy Spirit" (Matthew 28:19).

Jehovah's Witnesses and the Trinity

The trinitarian nature of God is imbedded in numerous passages throughout Scripture. Nevertheless, Jehovah's Witnesses tirelessly point out that the word *Trinity* is not found in the Bible (*Reasoning from the Scriptures* 406). The book *Let God Be True* describes the teaching of the Trinity as "a fundamental doctrine of the so-called 'Organized Religion' . . . such a doctrine, with the explanation thereof, is very confusing, and to excuse it with the word 'mystery' is not satisfying, . . . Satan is the originator of the 'trinity' doctrine" (81-2). In the 1936 publication *Riches,* the doctrine of the Trinity is attacked in this manner:

> Another lie made and told by Satan for the purpose
> of reproaching God's name and turning men away
> from God is that of the "trinity." That doctrine is
> taught by the religionists of "Christendom" and is in

62

substance this: 'That there are three gods in one;
God the Father, God the Son, and God the Holy
Ghost, all equal in power, substance and eternity.'
No man can explain that doctrine, because it is
false. That false doctrine was prominent in the
religions of ancient Babylon and Egypt and among
other mythologists, all of which are Devil religions.
(reproduced in Magnani 140)

In rejecting the doctrine of the Trinity, Jehovah's Witnesses
inaccurately define what the doctrine is: "The doctrine, in
brief, is that there are three gods in one: God the Father, God
the Son, and God the Holy Ghost" (*Let God Be True* 81). The
actual doctrine is that there are three divine persons in one God.
Nevertheless, the Society goes on to push its misrepresentation
to the point of mockery: "God-fearing persons who want to
know Jehovah and serve him find it a bit difficult to love and
worship a complicated, freakish-looking, three-headed God"
(*Let God Be True* 83).

Having misrepresented the doctrine as teaching that there
are three gods, Witnesses then appeal to Bible passages that
speak of the oneness of God. *What Do You Really Know About
God?* raises the question, "Who is God? Is he three gods in
one—a trinity?" and proceeds to answer, "No, the Bible says
'there is actually one God the Father.'—1 Corinthians 8:6"
(reproduced in Magnani 142).

The more one reads in Watchtower literature, the more a
definite pattern stands out. Over and over again, Watchtower
interpretation of the Bible is based on human reason; the title
of one of its standard Bible study books says as much—
Reasoning from the Scriptures. Rather than letting difficult
passages stand, the Jehovah's Witness tendency is to explain
away—or translate away!—what is not reasonable. When two
biblical texts at first seem to conflict with one another, rather

than dealing with the paradox, the Watchtower approach is to reject the one that is more difficult or unreasonable. The following excerpt from *Reasoning from the Scriptures* exemplifies this trait:

> At Genesis 1:1 the title "God" is translated from *'Elohim'*, which is plural in Hebrew. Trinitarians construe this to be an indication of the Trinity. They also explain Deuteronomy 6:4 to imply the unity of members of the Trinity when it says, "The LORD our God [from *'Elohim'*] is one LORD."
>
> The plural form of the noun here in Hebrew is the plural of majesty or excellence. (See *NAB* [*New American Bible*], St. Joseph Edition, Bible Dictionary, p. 330; also, *New Catholic Encyclopedia,* 1967, Vol. V, p. 287.) It conveys no thought of plurality of persons within a godhead. In similar fashion, at Judges 16:23 when reference is made to the false god Dagon, a form of the title *'elohim'* is used; the accompanying verb is singular, showing that reference is to just the one god. At Genesis 42:30, Joseph is spoken of as the "lord" (*'adho.neh'*, the plural of excellence) of Egypt.

Joseph's being called lord (plural) is an example of the plural of majesty or excellence. The case of the god Dagon is interesting in that upon the capture of the mighty Samson, the Philistine rulers exclaimed, "Our god has delivered Samson, our enemy into our hands," and then the people echoed, "Our god has delivered our enemy into our hands" (Judges 16:24). The Philistines were gloating over their capture of Samson and, by extension, the victory of their god over his. They may well have been mimicking the Hebrew expression. Eventually, of course, Samson, empowered by God, brought down the temple of Dagon (Judges 16:29,30).

The fact remains that the word *elohim* is used as more than a "plural of excellence," as we have seen in Genesis chapter 1. Moreover, already in the Old Testament, the LORD God manifested himself in human form, speaking both as the Lord and as a man. This is seen in Genesis chapter 18, when three men appeared to Abraham and spoke as the LORD. It was God and two men or angels.

The Jehovah's Witness account continues:

> The Greek language does not have a 'plural of majesty or excellence.' So, at Genesis 1:1 the translators of *LXX* [Greek *Septuagint* version] used *ho Theos'* (God, singular) as the equivalent of *'Elohim'*. At Mark 12:29, where a reply of Jesus is reproduced in which he quoted Deuteronomy 6:4, the Greek singular *ho Theos'* is similarly used. . . . At Deuteronomy 6:4, the Hebrew text contains the Tetragrammaton twice, and so should more properly read: "Jehovah our God is one Jehovah." (*NW*) [*New World* translation] The nation of Israel, to whom that was stated, did not believe, in the Trinity. The Babylonians and the Egyptians worshiped triads of gods, but it was made clear to Israel that Jehovah is different.

The use of *elohim* in Deuteronomy fits with the word for one; the Hebrew word (*echad*) allows for the concept of diversity in unity. It is the word used, for example, in Genesis 2:24, where the man and the woman together "become one flesh."

Any "trinity" the Babylonians and Egyptians may have worshiped was far removed from the biblical Trinity. Nor does it explain why the Christian church, rooted in the Bible, would centuries later and far removed from those influences adopt a pagan notion as its own. Without making the many connections necessary to prove its contention, the Watchtower claims that such pagan notions were introduced into Christendom by the philosophy of Plato *(Jehovah's Witnesses: Proclaimers of God's Kingdom* 36). Yet for the sake of argument, even granting that others had some concept of a trinity only serves to underscore the reality of the plurality within the Godhead, a truth that in pagan nations had deteriorated into false notions of three or more distinct gods.

The Jehovah's Witness presentation continues:

> If a passage can grammatically be translated in more than one way, what is the correct rendering? One that is in agreement with the rest of the Bible. If a person ignores other portions of the Bible and builds his belief around a favorite rendering of a particular verse, then what he believes really reflects, not the Word of God, but his own ideas and perhaps those of another imperfect human. (415-6)

For Jehovah's Witnesses, "agreement with the rest of the Bible" means agreement with their doctrinal bias. The fact is that the Bible speaks of God in two ways—as a single deity and as distinct persons. Rather than rule out one side of the picture, true biblical scholarship lets both stand as two aspects of the same truth.

The Watchtower's *Reasoning from the Scriptures* asks, "In what position does belief in the Trinity put those who cling to it?" and proceeds to answer its own question:

> It puts them in a very dangerous position. The evidence is indisputable that the dogma of the Trinity is not found in the Bible, nor is it in harmony with what the Bible teaches . . . It grossly misrepresents the true God . . .
>
> Regarding the Trinity, the Athanasian Creed (in English) says that its members are "incomprehensible." Teachers of the doctrine often state that it

is a "mystery." Obviously such a Trinitarian God is not the one that Jesus had in mind when he said: "We worship what we know." (John 4:22, *RS* [*Revised Standard Version*]) Do you really know the God you worship? (424-5)

Knowing God is not synonymous with comprehending him. We can know many people—even know them well—and yet not be privy to their inmost thoughts and feelings. How much more is that the case with God, who declares, "As the heavens are higher than the earth, so are my ways higher than your ways and my thoughts than your thoughts" (Isaiah 55:9).

The Holy Spirit

Since there is no Trinity in Watchtower thinking, it follows that the Father, the Son, and the Holy Spirit are not three distinct persons of the Godhead. If that is the case, then who, or what, is the Holy Spirit? For Jehovah's Witnesses, the Holy Spirit is an impersonal force: "The Holy Scriptures themselves unite to show that God's holy spirit is not a person but is God's *active force* by which he accomplishes his purpose and executes his will" (*Aid to Bible Understanding* 1543, emphasis in original). The publication *Holy Spirit* adds, "From God there goes forth an invisible active force by means of which he gets his will done. . . . It is a force that is operative, and it issues forth from God who is holy, that is to say, absolutely clean and righteous. He sends it forth to accomplish what is holy. So it is correctly called 'holy spirit'" (reproduced in Magnani 229).

In answer to the question, What is the Holy Spirit? *Reasoning from the Scriptures* offers a lengthy answer, which begins: "A comparison of Bible texts that refer to the holy spirit shows that it is spoken of as 'filling' people; they can be 'baptized' with it; and they can be 'anointed' with it. (Luke 1:41; Matt. 3:11; Acts 10:38) None of these expressions would be appropriate if the holy spirit were a person."

According to Ephesians 1:23 and 4:10, Christ "fills everything in every way" and he has ascended "in order to fill the whole universe." Does that mean Jesus is not a person?

By Witness reasoning, since water used in Baptism is not a person, then the Holy Spirit placed parallel to water must not be a person either. The fallacy of such reasoning can be seen in a parallel example: We are baptized into Christ and into his death (Romans 6:3). Since death, which is not a person, is set parallel to Christ, does that mean he is not a person?

As for being anointed by the Holy Spirit, this refers to oil being poured out in the act of anointing. Along the same lines, Witnesses appeal to Joel 2:28, "I will pour out my Spirit" to refute the personhood of the Holy Spirit. Yet the apostle Paul speaks of himself as being "poured out" (2 Timothy 4:6). Does that make Paul something impersonal?

Reasoning from the Scriptures continues:

> Jesus also referred to the holy spirit as a "helper" (Greek, *pa.ra'kle.tas*), and he said that this helper would "teach," "bear witness," "speak," and "hear." (John 14:16,17,26; 15:26; 16:13) It is not unusual in the Scriptures for something to be personified. For example, wisdom is said to have "children." (Luke 7:35) Sin and death are spoken of as being kings. (Rom 5:14,21) While some texts say that the spirit "spoke," other passages make clear that this was done through angels or humans. (Acts 4:24,25; 28:25; Matt. 10:19,20 compare Acts 20:23 with 21:10,11). . . .
>
> The correct identification of the holy spirit must fit *all the scriptures* that refer to that spirit. With this viewpoint, it is logical to conclude that the holy spirit is the active force of God. It is not a person but is a powerful force that God causes to emanate from himself to accomplish his holy will. (380-1)

While admitting that a number of texts point to the personhood of the Spirit, the Society falls back on what is "logical." Again, rather than letting the various texts stand by themselves, the organization forces them all to fit its notion of what they should say.

On the other hand, when it comes to Satan, the Society argues that the devil is a person, not just a personification. A 1973 *Awake!* article says, "Both Jehovah God and Jesus Christ are persons. Can an unintelligent 'force' carry on a conversation with a person? Also, the Bible calls Satan a manslayer, a liar, a father (in a spiritual sense) and a ruler. (John 8:44; 14:30) Only an intelligent person could fit all those descriptions" (reproduced in Magnani 230). The same arguments can be applied to the Holy Spirit. As the following passages concerning the Holy Spirit demonstrate, "only an intelligent person could fit all those descriptions."

He teaches: [Jesus said,] "But the Counselor, the Holy Spirit, whom the Father will send in my name, will teach you all things and will remind you of everything I have said to you" (John 14:26).

He is a teacher and comforter: [Jesus said,] "But I tell you the truth: It is for your good that I am going away. Unless I go away, the Counselor will not come to you; but if I go, I will send him to you. . . . But when he, the Spirit of truth, comes, he will guide you into all truth. He will not speak on his own; he will speak only what he hears, and he will tell you what is yet to come" (John 16:7,13).

He may be lied to: "Then Peter said, 'Ananias, how is it that Satan has so filled your heart that you have lied to the Holy Spirit and have kept for yourself some of the money you received for the land?'" (Acts 5:3).

He speaks in the first person and can be obeyed: "While they were worshiping the Lord and fasting, the Holy Spirit said, 'Set apart for me Barnabas and Saul for the work to which I have called them'" (Acts 13:2).

He knows the future: "Coming over to us, he [Agabus] took Paul's belt, tied his own hands and feet with it and said, 'The Holy Spirit says, "In this way the Jews of Jerusalem will bind the owner of this belt and will hand him over to the Gentiles"'" (Acts 21:11).

He has a mind and prays: "He who searches our hearts knows the mind of the Spirit, because the Spirit intercedes for the saints in accordance with God's will" (Romans 8:27).

He loves: "I urge you, brothers, by our Lord Jesus Christ and by the love of the Spirit, to join me in my struggle by praying to God for me" (Romans 15:30).

He searches and knows: "The Spirit searches all things, even the deep things of God. For who among men knows the thoughts of a man except the man's spirit within him? In the same way no one knows the thoughts of God except the Spirit of God" (1 Corinthians 2:10,11).

He has a will: "All these are the work of one and the same Spirit, and he gives them to each one, just as he determines" (1 Corinthians 12:11).

He may be grieved: "Do not grieve the Holy Spirit of God, with whom you were sealed for the day of redemption" (Ephesians 4:30).

The Jehovah God of the Jehovah's Witnesses is not the LORD God of the Scripture. Like the Bible's God, the Watchtower's Jehovah created the heavens and earth but again with some differences. Witnesses have tended to reject the theory of evolution (see the Watchtower publication *Did Man Get Here by Evolution or by Creation?*), but they allow for the days of Genesis chapter 1 to be longer periods of time. In keeping with their end-time chronology (chapter 8), they have seen each of the days of creation as 7,000 years. According to their chronology, we are now some 6,000 years into the seventh day, and soon the final 1,000 years (the millennium) will arrive and usher in the end of the last day. (See Penton 196-7.)

Typical of Watchtower doctrines, however, that of creation

has done some shifting over the years. While the book *Did Man Get Here by Evolution or by Creation?* refers to "man's creation nearly 6,000 years ago" (112), a recent issue of *Awake!* says that "the universe, including our planet Earth, was in existence *before* the creative days began," allowing for millions and billions of years (September 2006, 19).

Of special interest in the Society's system is the first creation of Jehovah God—the archangel Michael, also known as Jesus Christ. This is the next subject in our study.

6. Jehovah's Witnesses and Jesus
(1): Who Is Christ?

This One [Jesus] was not Jehovah God, but was "existing in the form of God". How so? He was a spirit person, just as "God is a spirit"; he was a mighty one, although not almighty as Jehovah God is; also he was before all others of God's creatures, because he was the first son that Jehovah God brought forth. For this reason he is called "the only begotten Son" of God, for God had no partner in bringing forth his first begotten Son. He was the first of Jehovah God's creations. (*Let God Be True* 34-5)

"What do you think about the Christ?" Jesus asked about himself. "Whose son is he?" (Matthew 22:42). These are the towering questions for all time. Who is Jesus Christ? According to the Bible and Christian doctrine through the ages, Jesus Christ is both the Son of God and Son of Man, that is, true God and true man.

Jesus Christ—God and Man

Already in the Old Testament prophecies, the coming Savior, the Messiah, was depicted as both divine and human. In the first gospel promise, given to Adam and Eve immediately after the fall into sin, God foretold that one of the descendants of Eve would crush the head of the tempter, thus displaying superhuman power; but he would also be struck in his heel, that is, wounded in the process: "So the LORD God said to the serpent, '. . . I will put enmity between you and the woman, and between your offspring and hers; he will crush your head, and you will strike his heel'" (Genesis 3:14,15).

The Old Testament goes on to teach that the Messiah would be a man and more than a mere man. To cite a passage from the prophet Isaiah: "For to us a child is born, to us a son is given, and the government will be on his shoulders. And he will be called Wonderful Counselor, Mighty God, Everlasting Father, Prince of Peace" (Isaiah 9:6). Although Christ's kingdom is not worldly, it is eternal: "Of the increase of his government and peace there will be no end" (9:7). In his celebrated chapter dealing with the sufferings and glories of the Savior (52:13–53:12), Isaiah spoke of the coming Messiah in a twofold manner, both as being "raised and lifted up and highly exalted" (52:13) and as having his appearance "disfigured beyond that of any man" (52:14).

A Thumbnail Sketch of the Two Natures in Christ

True God:

"In the beginning was the Word [Jesus], and the Word was with God, and the Word was God." (John 1:1)

"Thomas said to him, 'My Lord and my God!'" (John 20:28)

"[Jesus] through the Spirit of holiness was declared with power to be the Son of God by his resurrection from the dead." (Romans 1:4)

True Man:

"And she [Mary] gave birth to her firstborn, a son [Jesus]." (Luke 2:7)

"The Son of Man came to seek and to save what was lost." (Luke 19:10)

"When Jesus had cried out again in a loud voice, he gave up his spirit." (Matthew 27:50)

This divine-human nature was also evident during the earthly life of Jesus Christ, as recorded in the four gospels and throughout the New Testament. As a man, he was born, grew up, ate and drank, was hungry and thirsty, spoke of the Father as "greater than I" (John 14:28), and died. Yet Jesus also referred to himself as God. He performed miracles, spoke with divine authority, referred to himself as the Son of God as well as son of man, and rose from the dead. In stating, "Before Abraham was born, I am!" (John 8:58), Jesus was making a clear reference to the name by which God called himself, when speaking to Moses, "I AM WHO I AM" (Exodus 3:14). Jesus said to his disciples, "Anyone who has seen me has seen the Father" (John 14:9).

In resisting the devil's temptation to worship him, Jesus quoted Scripture, "For it is written: 'Worship the Lord your God, and serve him only'" (Matthew 4:10). Nevertheless, there were many times when people "worshiped" Jesus, and he never corrected them. On one such occasion, "a ruler came and knelt before him" (literally, "worshiped him"), asking Jesus to raise his daughter who had just died. Jesus responded to the man's worship and raised the girl (Matthew 9:18-26).

Both Old and New Testaments, then, speak of the Messiah in human and in divine terms, as when, for example, he is referred to as Immanuel, "God with us" (Isaiah 7:14; Matthew 1:23).

Unbelievers have consistently ridiculed the notion that God could have a Son. Yet the Bible uses the word *son* in other ways besides that of a physical male child, the product of sexual union. The term *son* refers to one who has certain characteristics. Barnabas, for example, means "son of encouragement," not because Encouragement was his father's name but because that was his nature. The Hebrew expression "son of man" is generally simply rendered "man." Zechariah 4:14 refers to "sons of fresh oil"; that means they were priests, who were involved in anointing with oil. Similarly the Bible speaks of those who are suffering as sons of affliction (Proverbs 31:5), those with tempestuous natures as sons of thunder (Mark 3:17), and so on.

In having the special designation, the Son of God, Jesus is "in very nature God" (Philippians 2:6). Believers become "sons of God through faith in Christ Jesus" (Galatians 3:26); but only Jesus is *the* Son of God, as he himself puts it, the "only begotten," or "one and only" (Greek: *monogenes*), Son of God (John 3:16).

Jehovah's Witnesses and Jesus

In spite of the biblical evidence as to the divinity of Jesus, the Watchtower rejects the historic Christian doctrine and attempts to explain away the above passages as well as many others.

Jehovah's Witnesses recognize that Jesus was miraculously born of the virgin Mary: "Jehovah took the perfect life of his only-begotten Son and transformed it from heaven to the egg cell in the womb of the unmarried girl Mary" (*From Paradise Lost to Paradise Regained* 127). They also acknowledge that Jesus was "a perfect human" (*Reasoning from the Scriptures* 306).

Yet as far as they are concerned, he is not God in the flesh. Rather, he was "the first and direct creation of Jehovah God" (*The Kingdom Is at Hand*, quoted in Martin, *Kingdom of the Cults* 53). As Jehovah's first creation and his "only begotten Son," Jesus was involved in creating all other things (*Aid to Bible Understanding* 390-1).

According to Jehovah's Witness teaching, rather than being the eternally begotten Son of God, Jesus was Michael the archangel who became a man (*Watchtower*, May 15, 1963, 307). Witnesses appeal to 1 Thessalonians 4:16 to say Jesus was Michael the archangel, since he will return at the end of the world with the voice of the archangel: "For the Lord himself will come down from heaven, with a loud command, with the voice of the archangel and with the trumpet call of God, and the dead in Christ will rise first."

According to the *Watchtower:* "When Jesus was on earth as a man, he was a Hebrew, and now in his capacity as Jehovah's royal Executioner he is called by the Hebrew name Abad'don, which means Destruction. (Job 26:6; 28:22; 31:12; 12:23; 14:19) In the Greek in which the inspired Christian Scriptures were written his similar title is Apollyon, which means Destroyer" (December 1, 1961, 719). While Jesus is recognized by such special designations, the Society denies his full divinity. *You Can Live Forever in Paradise on Earth* says, " 'But isn't Jesus called a god in the Bible?' someone may ask. This is true. Yet Satan is also called a god. (2 Corinthians 4:4)" (40).

A recent issue of the *Watchtower* sums up the organization's view: "Jesus Christ is, not Almighty God, but the Son of God" (July 1, 2006, 5).

Study the Scriptures

Jesus says, "You diligently study the Scriptures, because you think that by them you possess eternal life. These are the Scriptures that testify about me" (John 5:39). To examine every Bible passage about Jesus that Jehovah's Witnesses have twisted to fit their position would take an entire book. Indeed, some excellent volumes have been written on the Watchtower use of Scripture, among them *Reasoning from the Scriptures with the Jehovah's Witnesses* by Ron Rhodes and *Jehovah's Witnesses Answered Verse by Verse* by David A. Reed. The following is a selection of verses that commonly come up in discussions regarding the person of Jesus Christ.

Old Testament Passages

Exodus 6:2,3: "God also said to Moses, 'I am the LORD. I appeared to Abraham, to Isaac and to Jacob as God Almighty, but by my name the LORD I did not make myself known to them.'"

Like many other Old Testament passages, this one points to Jesus, although in an indirect way. The passage states that God had appeared to Abraham, Isaac, and Jacob, yet Jesus says that no man has seen the Father at any time: "No one has seen the Father except the one who is from God; only he has seen the Father" (John 6:46). Whom were the patriarchs seeing if it was God Almighty, but not God the Father? The obvious answer is Jesus, the second person of the Trinity.

Isaiah 9:6: "For unto us a child is born, to us a son is given, and the government will be on his shoulders. And he will be called Wonderful Counselor, Mighty God, Everlasting Father, Prince of Peace."

Arguing that Jesus is referred to as Mighty God and not God Almighty, *Reasoning from the Scriptures* says:

> At Isaiah 43:10 Jehovah says: "Before me no god was formed, nor shall there be any after me." Does

this mean that, because Jesus Christ is prophetically called "Mighty God" at Isaiah 9:6, Jesus must be Jehovah? Again, the context answers, No! None of the idolatrous Gentile nations formed a god before Jehovah, because no one existed before Jehovah. Nor would they at a future time form any real live god that was able to prophesy. (Isa. 46:9,10) But that does not mean that *Jehovah* never caused to exist anyone who is properly referred to as a god. . . At Isaiah 10:21 Jehovah is referred to as "mighty God," just as Jesus is in Isaiah 9:6; but only Jehovah is ever called "God *Almighty.*"—Gen. 17:1. (413-4, italics in original)

This labored distinction between Mighty God and God Almighty strikes one as grasping for straws, but it is the type of argument the Society resorts to in trying to discredit every biblical reference to the full divinity of Jesus. Witnesses are driven to the position that Jesus is mighty God but not *the* almighty God.

Isaiah 43:10,11: "'You are my witnesses,' declares the LORD, 'and my servant whom I have chosen. . . . I, even I, am the LORD, and apart from me there is no savior.'" The passage from which Jehovah's Witnesses derive their name (43:10) is immediately followed by a verse asserting that aside from the LORD God there is no savior. If there is no savior besides God, then how can Jesus, a created thing, be the savior? For the New Testament declares, "She [Mary] will give birth to a son, and you [Joseph] are to give him the name Jesus [which means, the LORD saves], because he will save his people from their sins" (Matthew 1:21).

Only God can forgive sins, and only God provides the means for our forgiveness—namely, the sacrificial death of Jesus. When Christ forgave the sins of the crippled man whom he healed, Jesus simply said, "Son, your sins are forgiven" (Mark 2:5). Jesus did not speak on behalf of God, but as God.

New Testament Passages

Mark 13:32 (also *Matthew 24:36*): "No one knows about that day and hour, not even the angels in heaven, nor the Son, but only the Father."

Like other religions that reject the Trinity, Jehovah's Witnesses point to passages in the gospels in which Jesus speaks of his humanity. This is one such passage. Arguing as to Jesus' limited knowledge, *Reasoning from the Scriptures* says:

> Mark 13:32, *RS* [*Revised Standard Version*]: "Of that day or that hour no ones knows, not even the angels in heaven, nor the Son, but only the Father." (Of course, that would not be the case if Father, Son, and Holy Spirit were coequal, comprising one Godhead. And if, as some suggest, the Son was limited by his human nature from knowing, the question remains, Why did the Holy Spirit not know?) (409)

Witnesses like to use other translations in addition to their *New World Translation* in their study books. This gives the impression of wide-ranging scholarship and of agreement of outside scholars with their conclusions.

As God and man, Jesus was both almighty and susceptible to weakness (such as hunger, weariness); he was also both all-knowing and yet limited in knowledge. Both the human and divine natures were evident at different times in his ministry. Ron Rhodes notes, "In this passage, Jesus was speaking from the vantage point of his humanity" (*Reasoning from the Scriptures with the Jehovah's Witnesses* 155-6).

Elsewhere he displayed his divine knowledge, as when John comments, "He did not need man's testimony about man, for he knew what was in a man" (John 2:25), or when the disciples observed, "Now we can see that you know all things" (John 16:30).

As for "only the Father" (Matthew 24:36) knowing, this need not exclude the Holy Spirit. As we noted in the previous chapter, the Bible says that "no one knows the thoughts of God except the Spirit of God" (1 Corinthians 2:11). Jesus might have said, "Only the Father knows, and of course that means the Spirit as well, since he alone knows the thoughts of God." But he chose not to say all that, and if Jehovah's Witnesses want to think the Trinity is thus overthrown, let them think it.

1 Corinthians 1:2: "To the church of God in Corinth, to those sanctified in Christ Jesus and called to be holy, together with all those everywhere who call on the name of our Lord Jesus Christ—their Lord and ours."

The phrase "call on the name of the Lord" is used in the Old Testament only in reference to God, never anyone else; for instance, Psalm 116:4 states, "Then I called on the name of the LORD: 'O LORD, save me!'" Yet the New Testament Greek equivalent of the phrase (used in the ancient Septuagint translation) is here applied to Jesus. Saint Paul was equating the Lord (Greek *Kyrios*) Jesus with the LORD (Hebrew YHWH) of the Old Testament Scriptures.

1 Corinthians 8:6: "Yet for us there is but one God, the Father, from whom all things came and for whom we live; and there is but one Lord, Jesus Christ, through whom all things came and through whom we live."

Witnesses like the first part of this verse, "there is actually to us one God, the Father" (*New World Translation*), since it seems to say that only the Father is God. But even their own translation cannot avoid the clear wording of the second part of the verse, "and there is one Lord, Jesus Christ." Does that mean that God the Father is not Lord? "Of course, the JW does not want to reach this conclusion," notes Reed, "because he always speaks of Jehovah as 'Lord'" (*Jehovah's Witnesses Answered Verse by Verse* 96). In fact, the two terms go together, as when Thomas exclaimed to Jesus, "My Lord and my God!" (John 20:28).

1 Corinthians 11:3: "Now I want you to realize that the head of every man is Christ, and the head of the woman is man, and the head of Christ is God."

Witnesses appeal to passages such as this in order to refute Jesus' divinity (see Kern 26-29). Arguing against Jesus being equal with God, *Reasoning from the Scriptures* takes up the comparison of Christ's relationship with the Father to that between a husband and wife:

> 1 Cor. 11:3, RS: "I want you to understand that the head of every man is Christ, the head of a woman is her husband, and the head of Christ is God." (Clearly, then, Christ is not God, and God is of superior rank to Christ. It should be noted that this was written about 55 C.E., some 22 years after Jesus returned to heaven. So the truth here stated applies to the relationship between God and Christ in heaven.) (410)

While the passage speaks of roles, it does not support the Watchtower belief that Jesus was a created angel. Reed comments:

> Within the human family, the head of the woman is the man. Does that mean that women are a lower form of life than men? Are women inferior to me? Not at all! It is simply God's arrangement that someone act as head, and he has assigned that role to man. Likewise within the Godhead—the Father acts as head without diminishing the full deity of the Son. (*Jehovah's Witnesses Answered* 97)

1 Corinthians 15:28: "When he has done this, then the Son himself will be made subject to him who put everything under him, so that God may be all in all."

What applied in the previous passage applies here. Contrary to Jehovah's Witness belief, Jesus did not cease to be a man after his resurrection. (They claim he returned to his state as an angelic being.) He remains the God-man, as 1 Timothy 2:5 states, "For there is one God and one mediator between God and men, the man Christ Jesus." In his role as the reconciler between God and man, Jesus subjected himself to the Father's will. This is not to be taken as a sign of inferiority or being subordinate in being to the Father.

Philippians 2:6-11: "[Jesus], being in very nature God, did not consider equality with God something to be grasped, but made himself nothing, taking the very nature of a servant, being made in human likeness. And being found in appearance as a man, he humbled himself and became obedient to death—even death on a cross! Therefore God exalted him to the highest place and gave him the name that is above every name, that at the name of Jesus every knee should bow, in heaven and on earth and under the earth, and every tongue confess that Jesus Christ is Lord, to the glory of God the Father."

This passage clearly teaches the divinity of Christ, as well as his humanity. When he "made himself nothing," Christ humbled himself; it does not mean he ceased to be God, for that is impossible. The *New World Translation* tries to avoid the obvious reference to divinity and translates the first part of the passage in this way: "[Jesus], although he was existing in God's form, gave no consideration to a seizure, namely, that he should be equal to God." In other words, Jesus was not presumptuous and did not claim to be someone he wasn't. Yet the Greek is a present participle—"being," not a past "was existing"; it indicates an ongoing state of existence. What does it mean that he is in God's form, if not that he is, indeed, God?

The following quotation from *Reasoning from the Scriptures* includes the *New World Translation* rendering of the latter part of this passage and an accompanying attempt to explain away the reference to Christ's divinity:

> Phil., 2:9-11: "For this very reason also God exalted him [Jesus Christ] to a superior position and kindly gave him the name that is above every other name, so that in the name of Jesus every knee should bend of those in heaven and those on earth and those under the ground, and every tongue should openly acknowledge that Jesus Christ is Lord to the glory of God the Father . . ." (Notice that Jesus Christ is here shown to be different from God the Father and subject to Him.) (198)

Yes, Jesus is "different" and "subject to" God the Father regarding Christ's humanity. He is also God.

Colossians 1:15,16: "He is the image of the invisible God, the firstborn over all creation. For by him all things were created: things in heaven and on earth, visible and invisible, whether thrones or powers or rulers or authorities; all things were created by him and for him."

Jehovah's Witnesses contend that "firstborn" means first created. The following excerpts from *Reasoning from the Scriptures* are somewhat lengthy, but they are worth examining since they show the sophisticated arguments Witnesses enlist:

> Col. 1:15,16, *RS* [*Revised Standard Version*]: "He [Jesus Christ] is the image of the invisible God, the first-born of all creation; for in him all things were created, in heaven and on earth." In what sense is Jesus Christ "the first-born of all creation"? (1) Trinitarians say that "first-born" here means prime, most excellent, most distinguished; thus Christ would be understood to be, not part of creation, but the most distinguished in relation to those who were created. If that is so, and if the Trinity doctrine is true, why are the Father and the holy spirit not also said to be the firstborn of all creation? But the Bible applies this expression

only to the Son. According to the customary meaning of "firstborn," it indicates that Jesus is the eldest in Jehovah's family of sons.

Firstborn is not necessarily the equivalent of first-created. The following verses demonstrate that "firstborn" is a title of preeminence that is transferable. Speaking of the two sons of Joseph, Genesis 41:51,52 says, "Joseph named his firstborn Manasseh and said, 'It is because God has made me forget all my trouble and all my father's household.' The second son he named Ephraim and said, 'It is because God has made me fruitful in the land of my suffering.'" Even though strictly speaking, Manasseh was Joseph's firstborn son, God later referred to Ephraim as his firstborn: "I am Israel's father, and Ephraim is my firstborn son" (Jeremiah 31:9). Therefore, while the term could refer to the physical firstborn, it was also used to indicate preeminence.

The Father and the Holy Spirit are not referred to as firstborn, since it was the Son who became incarnate and physically entered into the created world. The Witness article continues:

> (2) Before Colossians 1:15, the expression "the firstborn of" occurs upwards of 30 times in the Bible, and in each instance that it is applied to living creatures the same meaning applies—the firstborn is part of the group. "The firstborn of Israel" is one of the sons of Israel; "the firstborn of Pharaoh" is one of Pharaoh's family; "the firstborn of beast" are themselves animals. What, then, causes some to ascribe a different meaning to it at Colossians 1:15? Is it Bible usage or is it a belief to which they already hold and for which they seek proof?

As true man, Jesus is "part of the group" of humanity, its most illustrious member. Having never proven that

Christendom got its doctrine of the incarnation from some outside source, Witnesses simply assert that this supposedly satanic belief is being read into the text. Is it not more likely that they are reading in their own rationalistic ideas?

The Witness argument now turns to Christ's role in creation:

> (3) Does Colossians 1:16,17 (*RS*) exclude Jesus from having been created, when it says "In him all things were created . . . all things were created through him and for him"? The Greek word here rendered "all things" is *pan'ta,* an inflected form of *pas.* At Luke 13:2, *RS* renders this "all . . . other"; *JB* [*Jerusalem Bible*] reads "any other"; *NE* [*New English Bible*] says "anyone else." (See also Luke 21:29 in *NE* and Philippians 2:21 in *JB.*) In harmony with everything else that the Bible says regarding the Son, *NW* assigns the same meaning to *pan'ta* at Colossians 1:16,17 so that it reads, in part, "by means of him all *other things* were created . . . All *other things* have been created through him and for him." Thus he is shown to be a created being, part of the creation produced by God. (408-9)

The second point that Witnesses make with this passage is that Christ created and was before "all [other] things," adding the word *other* four times. Newer editions of the *New World Translation* have the word *other* in brackets, whereas older editions did not.

In either case, they argue that *other* is a legitimate addition to the text, since in Luke 13:2 most translations add the word to help clarify the meaning: "Do you think that these Galileans were worse sinners than all the *other* Galileans because they suffered this way?" (NIV, italics mine). There the text calls for the word *other* to clarify the reading and smooth it out. Yet in the Colossians passage, the word *other* is not necessary to clarify or smooth out the reading. It is only necessary if the translator has a preconceived idea of what the text should say. The bottom line is that Christ created all things, not *all other* things.

Colossians 2:9: "In Christ all the fullness of the Deity lives in bodily form."

This is another powerful verse attesting the divinity of Jesus. Once again, the Witnesses must explain it away. *Reasoning from the Scriptures* states:

> Admittedly, not everyone offers the same interpretation of Colossians 2:9. But what is in agreement with the rest of the inspired letter to the Colossians? Did Christ have in himself something that is his because he is God, part of a Trinity? Or is "the fullness" that dwells in him something that became his because of the decision of someone else? Colossians 1:19 (*KJ* [*King James Version*] Dy [*Challoner-Douay Version*]) says that all fullness dwelt in Christ because it "pleased the Father" for this to be the case. *NE* [*New English Bible*] says it was "by God's own choice."

In order to get around the fullness of God dwelling in Christ, Witnesses go back to an earlier verse in Colossians (1:19), which states that "God was pleased to have all his fullness dwell in him [Christ]." Such tactics accomplish nothing. For the text does not say that God the Father decided to implant divinity in Christ. A more literal translation would be "in him [Christ] all the fullness was pleased to dwell." God— not to the exclusion of the Son—decided upon and enacted the incarnation.

Reasoning from the Scriptures continues by shifting to another argument:

> According to Liddell and Scott's *Greek-English Lexicon, theo'tes* (the nominative form, from which *theo'te.tos* is derived) means "divinity, divine nature." (Oxford, 1968, p. 792) Being truly "divinity," or of "divine nature," does not make Jesus as the Son of God coequal and coeternal with the Father, any more than the fact that all humans share "humanity" or "human nature" makes them coequal or all the same age. (420-1)

This is weak. The fact that all human beings share in humanity *does* make them all equally human. An old man, a king, a beggar, and a child are all equally human. Along with the Father and the Holy Spirit, Jesus is equally God.

Hebrews 1:3: "The Son is the radiance of God's glory and the exact representation of his being, sustaining all things by his powerful word. After he had provided purification for sins, he sat down at the right hand of the Majesty in heaven."

Even the *New World Translation* translates ". . . the exact representation of his [God's] very being." How is Jesus, who is supposedly only a created being, God's "exact representation"? Since Jesus is both man and God, he can be and is the exact representation of God's nature.

The Cult Awareness and Research Ministry points out, "If the JW Jesus was first an angel and became a man, then the angel stopped being angelic in nature, changed natures, became a man, and he yet was the 'exact representation' of God? How is that so?"

2 Peter 1:1: "Simon Peter, a servant and apostle of Jesus Christ, to those who through the righteousness of our God and Savior Jesus Christ have received a faith as precious as ours." This passage refers to Jesus as "our God and Savior." The *New World Translation* tries to skirt around the obvious reference to Christ's divinity by translating "our God and [the] Savior Jesus Christ," as if "our God" is one individual and "the Savior" is another. The word *the* is not in the original Greek text.

Revelation 1:1; 3:14: "The revelation of Jesus Christ, which God gave him to show his servants what must soon take place. He made it known by sending his angel to his servant John. . . . To the angel of the church in Laodicea write: 'These are the words of the Amen, the faithful and true witness, the ruler of God's creation.'" The opening verse of the book of Revelation designates its author, Jesus, who according to his human nature, received the revelation from God. Jesus in turn sent an angel (messenger) to deliver it to John. Later (3:14), Jesus refers to himself as "the Amen, . . . the ruler of God's creation."

Reasoning from the Scriptures uses these verses to discredit the divinity of Christ:

> Rev. 1:1; 3:14, *RS:* "The revelation of Jesus Christ, which God gave him. . . . 'And to the angel of the church in Laodicea write: "The words of the Amen, the faithful and true witness, the beginning [Greek, *ar.khe'*] of God's creation."'" . . . Is that rendering correct? Some take the view that what is meant is that the Son was "the beginner of God's creation," that he was its "ultimate source." But Liddell and Scott's *Greek-English Lexicon* lists "beginning" as its first meaning of *arkhe'.* (Oxford, 1968, p. 252) The logical conclusion is that the one being quoted at Revelation 3:14 is a creation, the first of God's creations, that he had a beginning . . . (409)

The Greek word *arche*—from which derive many English words, such as *architect*—can mean "beginning, origin, beginner, first cause, source, ruler, authority." While the immediate context might allow the Watchtower interpretation as "beginning," the wider context of Scripture calls for "ruler" or "beginner." The same John who penned this inspired text, wrote in his gospel, "Through him all things were made;

without him nothing was made that has been made" (1:3). (Surprisingly, the *New World Translation* has, "All things came into existence through him, and apart from him not even one thing came into existence.")

Later in Revelation, the same word occurs when God says, "I am the Alpha and the Omega, the Beginning [*arche*] and the End" (21:6), and Christ says, "I am the Alpha and the Omega, the First and the Last, the Beginning [*arche*] and the End" (22:13). Jehovah's Witnesses apply these passages to Jehovah God; certainly he is not a created being. (See Reed, *Answering Jehovah's Witnesses Verse by Verse* 102-3.) Yet this expression is clearly applied to Jesus in Revelation 2:8: "These are the words of him who is the First and the Last, who died and came to life again." In the Old Testament they, along with the act of creation, apply to the LORD (Jehovah): "I am the first and I am the last. My own hand laid the foundations of the earth, and my right hand spread out the heavens" (Isaiah 48:12,13). Who is the beginning and the end, the first and the last, the creator of all? The almighty God—who reveals himself in Jesus Christ, the Son.

By twisting these and many other passages, Jehovah's Witnesses go against Christ's directive "that all may honor the Son just as they honor the Father. He who does not honor the Son does not honor the Father, who sent him" (John 5:23). If we honor the Father as God, then we are to honor the Son in the same manner.

Jesus is true God and true man, as attested in many passages. Herbert Kern's fine introduction to the Jehovah's Witnesses includes a chart with Scripture references showing how Jehovah and Jesus share the names and titles, are worthy of the same honor, have the same qualities, and perform the same acts. To summarize the information:

> Names and Titles: Lord and God; King of kings
> and Lord of lords; (my) salvation; shepherd;
> Rock; the first and the last.

> Worthy of the Same Honor: multitudes of heaven (angels) worship; every knee will bow and every tongue will swear (confess); worthy to receive glory and honor and power; being served.
>
> Possessing the Same Qualities: unchangeable; holy; unsearchable; righteous; true and faithful witness; strength; light; hope; spring of (living) water; quenching the thirst of those who come to him.
>
> Performing the Same Acts: creating; redeeming; forgiving; hearing prayer; stilling the storm; promising to be with his people; knowing all things; searching the hearts of people; repaying (rewarding); disciplining those he loves; holding his people securely; judging. (Kern 18-21)

For Jehovah's Witnesses, perhaps most striking of all the parallels is that just as God declared in the Old Testament, "You are my witnesses" (Isaiah 43:10), so Jesus declares in the New Testament, "You will be my witnesses" (Acts 1:8).

Many more Scripture passages could be introduced, but this sampling represents the issues at stake. In the next chapter, before examining Christ's death and resurrection, we will focus on one specific book of the Bible, the gospel of John. Because of the numerous passages in the gospel of John dealing with the divinity of Jesus, this subject warrants a treatment all its own.

7. Jehovah's Witnesses and Jesus
(2): Denial of Full Divinity

> Jesus replied, ". . . Your father Abraham rejoiced at the thought of seeing my day; he saw it and was glad."
>
> "You are not yet fifty years old," the Jews said to him, "and you have seen Abraham!"
>
> "I tell you the truth," Jesus answered, "before Abraham was born, I am!" At this, they picked up stones to stone him, but Jesus hid himself, slipping away from the temple grounds. (John 8:54-59)

Although he lived on earth almost two thousand years ago, Jesus' life is well documented. In fact, its documentation is unprecedented in ancient history; there are not one or two or even three first-generation biographies of Christ, but four. Each bears witness to his life, death, and resurrection.

The first three gospels—Matthew, Mark, and Luke—are referred to as the synoptic gospels, a term denoting that they approach the life of Christ from much the same perspective.

That is, they "see together," as the word *synoptic* suggests. These gospels cover many of the same incidents and teachings from Jesus' life. The fourth gospel—that of John—was written later and adds unique perspectives to the life of Christ.

The Three States of Jesus

According to Jehovah's Witnesses, Jesus has existed in three different states:

1. Michael the archangel, God's first creation.

2. A perfect man on earth for 33 years.

3. After his resurrection, his return to being Michael the archangel.

The Gospel of John

The gospel of John omits much material that is in the synoptics, no doubt because John recognized that he need not repeat the same information again. Rather than cover the same ground, John's gospel introduces much material not found in the other three. Although all the gospels point to the divine-human nature of Christ, John emphasizes it. We might say that of the four gospels, his is the most theological. It emphasizes Christ's divinity.

This poses a problem for Jehovah's Witnesses, particularly in relation to several key passages. An examination of a number of passages from John's gospel, with special attention given to John 1:1, points out the divinity of Jesus and demonstrates the biased nature of the *New World Translation*.

John 1:1

John 1:1: "In the beginning was the Word, and the Word was with God, and the Word was God."

Any discussion of the Jehovah's Witness view of Jesus must include a review of John 1:1, probably the most famous—or infamous—passage in the *New World Translation*. According to that translation, the passage reads, "In [the] beginning the Word was, and the Word was with God, and the Word was a god." Almost all translations, such as the New International Version used in this book, translate, "the Word was God."

Why the discrepancy? After noting the very few translations that more or less agree with the Society's rendering of John 1:1 (some have "the Word was divine"), *Reasoning from the Scriptures* defends the Jehovah's Witness translation:

> What is it that these translators are seeing in the Greek text that moves some of them to refrain from saying "the Word was God"? The definite article (the) appears before the first occurrence of *the-os'* (God) but not before the second. The articular (when the article appears) construction of the noun points to an identity, a personality, whereas a singular anarthrous (without the article) predicate noun before the verb (as the sentence is constructed in Greek) points to a quality about someone. So the text is not saying that the Word (Jesus) was the same as the God *with whom* he was but, rather, that the Word was godlike, divine, a god. (212)

Commenting on John 1:1-3, the Witness publication *The Truth Shall Make You Free* asserts, "Does this mean that Jehovah God (*Elohim*) and the only begotten Son are two persons but at the same time one God and members of a so-called 'trinity' or 'triune god'? When religion so teaches it violates the Word of God, wrests the Scriptures to the destruction of those who are misled, and insults God-given intelligence and reason" (45).

Here as elsewhere, Witnesses have tried to draw upon the scholarly research of others to bolster their case, but as one scholar remarks, "The Watchtower article has, by judicious cutting, made me say the opposite of what I meant to say" (Bowman, "Whitewashing the Watchtower" 10).

Bruce Metzger, one of the premiere Greek scholars of the 20th century, commented on the Watchtower translation of John 1:1, which he referred to as "a frightful mistranslation" (75). Noting the argument that *theos* lacks the definite article, Metzger cites another grammarian—Dr. Ernest Colwell of the University of Chicago—who observed that when a noun precedes a verb, the Greek does not use the article. Metzger proceeds to turn the Witnesses' own argument against them:

> In a lengthy Appendix in the Jehovah's Witnesses' translation, which was added to support the mistranslation of John 1:1, there are quoted thirty-five other passages in John where the predicate noun has the definite article in Greek. These are intended to prove that the absence of the article in John 1:1 requires that θεος [*theos*, God] must be translated "a god." None of the thirty-five instances is parallel, however, for in every case the predicate noun stands *after* the verb, and so, according to Colwell's rule, properly has the article. So far, therefore, from being evidence against the usual translation of John 1:1, these instances add confirmation of the rule of the Greek definite article. (75-6)

Not everyone is interested in following these technicalities. Yet it is important to point them out from time to time, since it is with a show of scholarship that Watchtower literature has deceived many.

Using more lay-friendly terms, Robert Bowman Jr. shows that with the Greek word order, the phrase would be comparable to the English sentences "George was the king" or "George was king" ("Whitewashing" 10). One translation captures the idea of the wording by rendering it, "What God was the Word was" (10). Bowman goes on to suggest that "by not saying 'the Word was *the* God,' John avoided identifying the Word as God the Father" (11). This is similar to the wording of the ancient Athanasian Creed, "Such as the Father is, such is the Son, and such is the Holy Spirit."

In the opening phrase of John 1:1, the *New World Translation* properly has "In [the] beginning," even though the Greek has no article. Later, in the first chapter of John's gospel, the Greek word *theos* appears two more times without the article, and the *New World Translation* renders it, "No man has seen *God* at any time; the only begotten *god* who is in the bosom position with the Father is the one who has explained him" (verse 18, italics added). The New International Version has "No one has ever seen God, but God the One and Only [footnote: or the Only Begotten], who is at the Father's side, has made him known." It is obvious that the Jehovah's Witness translators have arbitrarily capitalized or lowercased and arbitrarily supplied "a" or not supplied it to fit their ideas of what they want the text to say.

As is so often the case, rather than let the biblical text stand as it is, the Jehovah's Witnesses appeal to what seems reasonable: "Certainly the apostle John was not so unreasonable as to say that someone ('the Word') was with some other individual ('God') and at the same time was that other individual" (*"The Word" Who Is He?* quoted in Martin, *Kingdom of the Cults* 53).

Indeed, it does not seem to make sense to say that the Word was with God and at the same time was God, even though that is what the text presents. Elsewhere, Witnesses drive home the point: "Also, verses 1, 2 say that in the beginning he was '*with* God.' Can one be *with* someone and at the same time *be* that person? At John 17:3, Jesus addresses the Father as 'the only true God'; so, Jesus as 'a god' merely reflects his Father's divine qualities" (*Reasoning from the Scriptures* 416). Yet that is exactly what John is saying. In fact, Jesus is *with* God and *is* God. This is not explained on the basis of reason, but in recognition that within the Godhead, Jesus is God and yet with God the Father and Spirit.

Not only does the refusal to acknowledge Jesus as God run into translation problems, but it also raises theological challenges to the Jehovah's Witness position. For one thing, if Jesus is "a" god, then isn't that polytheism, the belief in many gods? Yet the Bible—and Jehovah's Witness theology— teaches that there is only one true God (monotheism). The passage upon which Witnesses base their name, Isaiah 43:10, says, "'You are my witnesses,' declares the LORD [Jehovah], 'and my servant whom I have chosen, so that you may know and believe me and understand that I am he. Before me no god was formed, nor will there be one after me.'" (See also Isaiah 44:6,8.)

In other words, does Jesus being "a god," then, mean that he is a false god? If that were the case, he would certainly not be worthy of the honor that even the Jehovah's Witnesses acknowledge belongs to him. John 1:1 deals with the very nature of God when it says the Word was God. To say that in addition to God, the Word was "a" god suggests that there is more than one true God.

Other Passages From the Gospel of John

John 5:18: "For this reason the Jews tried all the harder to kill him; not only was he breaking the Sabbath, but he was even calling God his own Father, making himself equal with God."

The Jews of Jesus' day understood that he was equating himself with God. If that was not the case, and if he had meant something else, why did Jesus not try to correct their misunderstanding? Or if the evangelist John was merely reporting the error of the Jews' thinking and Jesus was not really God, then why did John not clarify the situation with an editorial comment?

On other occasions when he was misunderstood, Jesus did not hesitate to correct his detractors, as the following exchange demonstrates: "The Jews answered him, 'Aren't we right in saying that you are a Samaritan and demon-possessed?' 'I am not possessed by a demon,' said Jesus, 'but I honor my Father and you dishonor me'" (John 8:48,49). Toward the end of his gospel, John added an editorial comment about a misunderstanding among the disciples concerning a remark that the risen Christ made: "Jesus answered, 'If I want him [John] to remain alive until I return, what is that to you? You must follow me.' Because of this, the rumor spread among the brothers that this disciple would not die. But Jesus did not say that he would not die; he only said, 'If I want him to remain alive until I return, what is that to you?'" (21:22,23).

In the case of Christ's "making himself equal with God," there was no need for clarification from either Jesus or John. For that is exactly what Jesus meant.

John 8:58: "'I tell you the truth,' Jesus answered, 'before Abraham was born, I am!'" (To read more of the passage in context, refer to the passage at the beginning of this chapter.)

The *New World Translation* renders John 8:58: "Jesus said to them, 'Most truly I say to you, Before Abraham came into existence, I have been.'" In this case, the translation has to do with the tense of the Greek phrase *ego eimi*, "I am." The verb is not a past tense, as the Witnesses have rendered it. Jehovah's Witnesses used to argue that the verb is a "historical present" (Bowman, "Whitewashing" 11). This would be similar to what we might use when narrating an incident from the past while putting it into the present tense in order to make it more vivid: "So, then we get together and go to see . . ."

In more recent years, the term they have used has been "the present of past action" (Bowman, "Whitewashing" 12). Even if for the sake of argument that were the case, it would not solve the problem Jehovah's Witnesses have with this text. Why would John use the past tense for Abraham but not for

Jesus, if Jesus were simply saying that he, perhaps like the angels, somehow had an existence from ancient times? But John did not use two past tenses: "Before Abraham came into existence, I have been" (*New World Translation*). If that were the case, then why did the Jews want to kill Jesus? Later (in John 10:31), the Jews again wanted to kill Jesus, because he made himself out to be God by claiming, "I and the Father are one" (10:30).

What the Jehovah's Witness translation is trying to avoid is the obvious connection between Jesus' words and Exodus 3:14, in which God refers to himself as "I AM" (see chapter 3). Because he claimed to be God, the Jews thought Jesus was being blasphemous and worthy of death. The Jews who hated and eventually killed Jesus denied that Jesus was God; Jehovah's Witnesses agree with the unbelieving Jews that Jesus is not God.

John 14:8,9: "Philip said, 'Lord, show us the Father and that will be enough for us.' Jesus answered: 'Don't you know me, Philip, even after I have been among you such a long time? Anyone who has seen me has seen the Father. How can you say, "Show us the Father"?'"

The *New World Translation* of John 14:8,9 changes the meaning to deny the oneness of Jesus with the Father: "He that has seen me has seen the Father [also]." The word *also* is added, so that instead of Jesus saying that to see him is to see the Father, the two are treated separately. Regarding Jesus' designation as the Son of God, the Cult Awareness Research and Ministry asks the following telling questions:

> Does the term Son of God mean that Jesus is not God? If so, then does the term Son of Man mean that Jesus is not a man?
>
> If the term Son of God means that Jesus is a man, then what does the term Son of Man mean?
>
> If the term Son of Man means that Jesus is a man, then what does the term Son of God mean?

John 14:28: "You heard me say, 'I am going away and I am coming back to you.' If you loved me, you would be glad that I am going to the Father, for the Father is greater than I."

Jehovah's Witnesses argue that when Jesus says the Father is greater than he, that it means Jesus is not God. But this is not the case. Jesus was speaking of his position, not his nature. A husband is greater in authority than his wife, but they are equal in nature (see Ephesians chapter 6). As a man, Jesus was in a state of humility. Hebrews 2:9 declares, "But we see Jesus, who was made a little lower than the angels, now crowned with glory and honor because he suffered death, so that by the grace of God he might taste death for everyone." And as a man, Jesus was "born of a woman, born under law, to redeem those under law" (Galatians 4:4). Jesus was in a lower position because in order to save us from sin and death, he was a man as well as God. Jesus has two natures—human and divine. The incarnation answers the Watchtower's objections.

John 17:3: [Jesus said,] "Now this is eternal life: that they may know you, the only true God, and Jesus Christ, whom you have sent."

To Witnesses, John 17:3 means that the Father is the only true God. What then are we to make of Jude 4, which refers to Jesus as "our only Sovereign and Lord"? Does that exclude God the Father from being Sovereign and Lord? Because of the unity of God, such epithets apply to the individual person within the Godhead as well as to the Trinity. In Hebrews 1:8, God refers to the Son as God: "But about the Son he [God] says, 'Your throne, O God, will last for ever and ever.'"

This verse is especially striking since it immediately follows these words: "And again, when God brings his firstborn into the world, he says, 'Let all God's angels worship him.' In speaking of the angels he says, 'He makes his angels winds, his servants flames of fire'" (1:6,7). Contrary to the Watchtower notion that Jesus is a created angel, God here sets him in contrast to the angels, calling on them to worship him.

John 20:17: "Jesus said [to Mary Magdalene], 'Do not hold on to me, for I have not yet returned to the Father. Go instead to my brothers and tell them, "I am returning to my Father and your Father, to my God and your God."'"

Reasoning from the Scriptures comments on this verse, "so to the resurrected Jesus, the Father was God, just as the Father was God to Mary Magdalene. Interestingly, not once in Scripture do we find the Father addressing the Son as 'my God'" (212). As a man, Jesus referred to "my God." Since his relationship to the Father is different from other people, he did not say "our God" (Rhodes, *Reasoning from the Scriptures with the Jehovah's Witnesses* 152-3). Indeed, the Father never spoke of the Son as "my God," but then the Bible never refers to the Father as true man. The incarnation was the role of God the Son.

John 20:28. "Thomas said to him [Jesus], 'My Lord and my God!'"

Nothing could be more straightforward than these words of Thomas to the risen Christ. The text does not say, Thomas looked at Jesus and then took God's name in vain by exclaiming, "My Lord and my God." He said it *to* Jesus. The words are so direct that even the *New World Translation* has "Thomas said to him [Jesus], 'My Lord and my God!'"

Jesus' Resurrection and the Worship of Christ

In closing our discussion of the Jehovah's Witnesses and Jesus Christ, it is appropriate to take a brief look at two related topics: his resurrection from the dead and whether or not it is proper to worship him.

Jesus' Resurrection

According to Jehovah's Witness teaching, Jesus did not die on a cross but on a "torture stake" (a subject we will discuss in chapter 10). Not only did he not die on the cross, as Christians believe, but he did not rise from the dead in his physical body (*Awake!* July 22, 1973, 4). Such thinking goes back to the time of Charles Taze Russell, who declared in the 1899 *Studies in the Scriptures*, "The man Jesus is dead, forever dead" (reproduced in Magnani 110).

According to the Society, the man Jesus remains dead, but a spirit creature came forth from the tomb. *Let God Be True* says that Jesus "was not raised out of the grave a human creature, but he was raised a spirit" (272). *You Can Live Forever in Paradise on Earth* asserts that others will follow, since "he was the first to be raised as a spirit person" (172).

The Bible expressly attests to Jesus' physical resurrection; for example, when the disciples thought they were seeing a ghost, Jesus told them, "Why are you troubled, and why do doubts rise in your minds? Look at my hands and my feet. It is I myself! Touch me and see; a ghost does not have flesh and bones, as you see I have" (Luke 24:38,39). The Society challenges that: "We deny that He was raised in the flesh, and challenge any statement to that effect as being unscriptural" (*The Finished Mystery,* reproduced in Magnani 114). Thus, even Scripture becomes "unscriptural"!

Elsewhere the organization explains its position:

> Came the third day, Nisan 16, which was the day when the high priest offered the barley-harvest first-fruits to Jehovah at his temple. On that same day Almighty God brought forth a grander first-fruits by raising his faithful son Jesus Christ from the dead. The soldiers posted as a security guard at the tomb did not see Jesus raised from the dead. Why not? Because as the apostle Peter writes, in 1 Peter 3:18, "Christ died once for all time concerning sins, a righteous person for unrighteous ones, that he might lead you to God, he being put to death in the flesh, but being made alive in the spirit." Of course, the Roman soldiers could not

> see a spirit person; but they did see God's angel
> who materialized in glory and broke Pilate's seal
> and rolled away the stone . . . (*Babylon the Great
> Has Fallen* 423-4)

"Being made alive in the spirit" could refer to the Holy
Spirit (the Greek text does not distinguish between the capital
and lowercase letters as does the English). In other passages,
Christ's resurrection is attributed to the Father (e.g., Galatians
1:1) and to the Son himself (e.g., John 10:17,18). Even if "the
spirit" refers to Christ's own spirit, it does not eliminate the
physical resurrection, for (contrary to Watchtower doctrine)
human beings consist of a body and spirit. Whether or not the
guards saw Jesus is beside the point. The resurrected Jesus
was able to appear or disappear at will, as when he showed
himself to the disciples who had gathered behind closed
doors (John 20:19).

Nevertheless, in the world of the Watchtower organization,
the resurrected Christ was not—and is not—a real man. *You
Can Live Forever in Paradise on Earth* declares, "Having given
up his flesh for the life of the world, Christ could never take it
again and become a man once more" (143). The book goes on
to speculate that Jehovah removed the body from the tomb, for
if it remained there the disciples "could not have understood
that he had been raised from the dead, since at that time
they did not fully appreciate spiritual things" (144). Witness
literature points out that when Jesus appeared to his disciples,
it was not in his preresurrection body:

> Therefore the bodies in which Jesus manifested
> himself to his disciples after his return to life were
> not the body in which he was nailed to the tree.
> They were merely materialized for the occasion,
> resembling on one or two occasions the body in
> which he died, but on the majority of occasions
> being unrecognizable by his most intimate disciples.

> The body which was put in the sepulcher was dis-
> posed of without corruption according to God's
> prophecy and by his almighty power. (*The
> Kingdom Is at Hand*, reproduced in Magnani 115)

The occasional lack of recognition on the part of the disciples may be attributed to their surprise, their grief in thinking he was still dead, or God's temporarily withholding recognition.

Since he is no longer a human being but a spirit person, Witnesses believe that when the risen Christ returns, it will not be as a human being: "Christ Jesus comes, not again as a human, but as a glorious spirit person" (*Let God Be True* 185). According to Jehovah's Witnesses, then, Jesus has existed in three different states:

1. Michael the archangel, God's first creation.
2. A perfect man on earth for 33 years.
3. After his resurrection, his return to being Michael the archangel. (Kern 15)

Christians may be surprised to realize how foreign Jehovah's Witness beliefs concerning Jesus are to what might be called mainline Christianity. More significant, their beliefs are foreign to the Bible. One last example will serve—Jesus' own prediction of his physical resurrection from the dead: "Jesus answered them, 'Destroy this temple, and I will raise it again in three days.' The Jews replied, 'It has taken forty-six years to build this temple, and you are going to raise it in three days?' But the temple he had spoken of was his body" (John 2:19-21).

In regard to their beliefs about Christ's resurrection, the Jehovah's Witnesses are wrong.

The Worship of Christ

When tempted by Satan to bow down and worship him, Jesus responded by quoting from the Old Testament Scriptures: "Away from me, Satan! For it is written: 'Worship the Lord your God, and serve him only'" (Matthew 4:10). Yet

Jesus himself received worship from other people, something he certainly would have rejected were he not God. The example of Thomas is but one of many.

When Stephen, the first martyr, was about to die, he appealed to Jesus to receive his spirit (Acts 7:59). Yet Jehovah's Witnesses do not pray to Jesus and those guilty of worshiping Jesus are disfellowshiped. The *Watchtower* states, "It is unscriptural for worshipers of the living and true God to render worship to the Son of God, Jesus Christ" (November 1, 1964, 671).

In order to get around the scriptural difficulties, the *New World Translation* uses the expression "do obeisance to" instead of the usual translation "worship" for the Greek word for worship. In Hebrews 1:6, a passage we reviewed earlier in this chapter, older editions of the *New World Translation* have the angels being told to "worship" Jesus, but in newer editions that has been changed to "do obeisance to" him. No doubt Witness leaders regret the use of the word *worship* in regard to Jesus, but it is on record.

In recognition of Christ's special status, Jehovah's Witnesses are to bow down to Jesus. A 1945 article in the *Watchtower* declares, "Since Jehovah God now reigns as King by means of his capital organization Zion, then whoever would worship Him must also worship and bow down to Jehovah's Chief One in that capital organization, namely Jesus Christ, his Co-regent on the throne of The Theocracy" (reproduced in Magnani 164).

In Revelation 22:8,9, John relates how after he had received the contents of the book of Revelation, "I fell down to worship at the feet of the angel who had been showing them to me," only to be told by the angel, "Do not do it! I am a fellow servant with you and with your brothers the prophets and of all who keep the words of this book. Worship God!" In the confused theology of the Jehovah's Witnesses, they and the angels bow down to Jesus, a created angel. But they do not want to call it worship.

8. The End Times

You may say to yourselves, "How can we know when a message has not been spoken by the LORD?" If what a prophet proclaims in the name of the LORD does not take place or come true, that is a message the LORD has not spoken. That prophet has spoken presumptuously. Do not be afraid of him. (Moses, Deuteronomy 18:21,22)

The words are clear. If someone makes a false prophecy, after having claimed to be a prophet of God, then that person is a false prophet and is not to be listened to. Do Jehovah's Witnesses claim to be a prophet of God? Indeed, they claim to be *the* prophetic voice of God. Their organization is the only true church, and they are the only true voice for God in the world. In a 1972 article, referred to earlier in chapter 1, the *Watchtower* magazine declared (somewhat ironically, as it happened to be the April 1 issue):

So does Jehovah have a prophet to help them, to warn them of dangers and to declare things to come?

> These questions can be answered in the affirmative.
> Who is this prophet? . . . This "prophet" was not
> one man, but was a body of men and women. It
> was the small group of footstep followers of Jesus
> Christ, known at that time as International Bible
> Students. Today they are known as Jehovah's
> Christian Witnesses. . . . Of course, it is easy to say
> that this group acts as a "prophet" of God. It is
> another thing to prove it. (197)

But has the Watchtower been able to "prove it"? If they are God's true voice in these times, then what they say should prove to be true, especially in regard to prophecy, which was a foundation of the early organization and an integral part of their system throughout the years. The Society has focused much of its prophetic ministry on the end times, even though in speaking of the end of the world Jesus himself said, "No one knows about that day or hour" (Matthew 24:36).

When it comes to predicting the future, the Watchtower organization—going back to its founder—has repeatedly failed. What follows are some of the false predictions made over the years by the Watchtower organization.

Passages on the End Times

Time of Christ's return unknown:

"No one knows about that day or hour, not even the angels in heaven, nor the Son, but only the Father. Therefore keep watch, because you do not know on what day your Lord will come" (Matthew 24:36,42).

Time of Christ's return unexpected:

"Now, brothers, about times and dates we do not need to write to you, for you know very well that the day of the Lord will come like a thief in the night" (1 Thessalonians 5:1,2).

The Watchtower's False Prophecy

As noted in chapter 3, Charles Taze Russell's Bible studies were often devoted to Adventist-type ideas of the imminent return of Christ. In an early edition (1897) of his *Studies in the Scriptures,* Russell wrote, "But now we are in the end of this Gospel age, and the Kingdom is being established or set up. Our Lord, the appointed King, is now present, since October 1874, A.D., according to the testimony of the prophets, to those who have ears to hear; and the formal inauguration of his kingly office dates from April 1878 A.D." (Vol. 4, 621).

While declaring that Christ was invisibly present and setting up his kingdom on earth, Russell pointed ahead to the cataclysmic end of the present world in 1914.

1914: The Year of Christ's Return

In 1888, in *The Time Is at Hand,* Russell asserted that "the 'battle of the great day of God Almighty' (Rev. 16:14), which will end in A.D. 1914 with the complete overthrow of earth's present rulership, is already commenced. The gathering of the armies is plainly visible from the standpoint of God's Word" (1908 edition, Magnani 101). When World War I broke out in 1914, Russell declared in a sermon:

> The present great war in Europe is the beginning of the Armageddon of the Scriptures. (Rev. 16:16-20.) It will eventuate in the complete overthrow of all the systems of error which have so long oppressed the people of God and deluded the world. All iniquity of every kind will go down. The glorious Kingdom of Messiah is about to be set up in the earth, for the deliverance of the world and the establishment of permanent right-eousness. (Magnani 81)

The word *Armageddon* (literally, "mountain of Megiddo," a site in northern Israel) appears only in Revelation 16:16 and is figurative for the final battle between the forces of good and evil (Kern 46). In Jehovah's Witness literature, it is the great battle that will usher in the end of the old order and the beginning of paradise on earth.

In order to arrive at the date of October 1914, Russell and other students of the end times followed the lead of people like Nelson H. Barbour who had developed a complicated system of dating that was often based on figurative biblical numbers. They calculated a 2,520 year period, based on the "seven times" of Daniel (7 x 360 days [which symbolize years] = 2,520). Going back to the destruction of the temple in Jerusalem in 607 B.C., the predictors came up with the 1914 date (Kern 46). The Jehovah's Witness book *The Truth Shall Make You Free* explains their thinking:

> Inasmuch as the count of the Gentile "seven times" began its first year in the fall of 607 B.C. to the fall of B.C. 1 is exactly 606 years. From the fall of B.C. 1 to the fall of A.D. 1 is one year [sic; it would actually be two years, with the year 0 in between], do not forget. Hence from the fall of B.C. 1 to fall of A.D. 1914 is 1,914 years, and the sum total is 2,520 years, ending in the fall of A.D. 1914. By this method Jehovah, who is an accurate Timekeeper as to his purposes, symbolically foretold that the "times of the Gentiles", that is, the "seven times", would continue to the fall of A.D. 1914. Before that date, therefore, the true Theocratic Government of Messiah, which was foreshadowed by the typical Theocracy of Jerusalem, could not be set up. (239)

As it turns out, even if such calculations had any validity, they would have been based on a wrong starting date. Almost every Bible scholar sets the fall of Jerusalem and destruction of the temple of Solomon at 587/586 B.C., two decades later than the date used by the Russellites. (See, for example, Myers 990.)

In addition, the Russellites drew upon extra-biblical material that appeals to people's fascination with the mysterious and esoteric. Until 1928, their calculations even included measurements from the Great Pyramid in Egypt. Wrote Russell in *Thy Kingdom Come*, "The Pyramid witnesses that the close of 1914 will be the beginning of the time of trouble such as was not since there was a nation—nor ever shall be afterward" (Kern 44).

When all the calculations were in order, they also included the 144,000 true believers who were the "faithful and discreet slave" (Kern 42). This number has caused further complications in the Watchtower system, since at least some of these people would still be alive at the end of the present world. Today, all but a handful of that generation have died off.

When the Great War did not usher in Russell's "glorious kingdom of Messiah," adjustments needed to be made. The message was altered, and the official line was changed so that in 1914, Jesus became the invisible ruler of God's kingdom in heaven. This is the "good news" proclaimed by the Watchtower Society, God's "visible agency on earth" (Kern 8-9). Moreover, the organization began teaching that 1914 marked the beginning of the "last days," as the October 1, 1980, *Watchtower* puts it (19).

1925: The Year of the Return of Faithful Men of Old

Charles Taze Russell died in 1916, but his organization's penchant for prophecy did not. His successor, Judge Rutherford, took up where the founder had left off. Rather than concentrate on the return of Christ, however, Rutherford turned his attention to other Bible notables. In the publication *Millions Now Living Will Never Die,* Rutherford predicted that the biblical patriarchs and prophets would return to earth: "Therefore we may confidently expect that 1925 will mark the return of Abraham, Isaac, Jacob and the faithful prophets of old, particularly those named by the Apostle in Hebrews chapter 11, to the condition of human perfection" (published in 1918; quotation from the 1920 edition reproduced in Magnani 84-5).

In the years following, the *Watchtower* magazine took up the drumbeat. The September 1, 1922, edition declared, "The date 1925 is even more distinctly indicated by the Scriptures than 1914" (262), and the April 1, 1923, edition followed up, "Our thought is, that 1925 is definitely settled by the Scriptures. As to Noah, the Christian now has much more upon which to base his faith than Noah had upon which to base his faith in a coming deluge" (106).

Finally, when the year 1925 arrived, the tune began to change: "The year 1925 is here. With great expectation Christians have looked forward to this year. Many have confidently expected that all members of the body of Christ will be changed to heavenly glory during this year. This may be accomplished. It may not be. In his own due time God will accomplish his purposes concerning his people. Christians should not be so deeply concerned about what may transpire this year" (*Watchtower,* January 1, 1925, 3).

By September, the *Watchtower* was saying, "It is to be expected that Satan will try to inject into the minds of the consecrated, the thought that 1925 should see an end to the work, and that therefore it would be needless for them to do more" (262).

By August 1, 1926, the *Watchtower* message was, "Some anticipated that the work would end in 1925, but the Lord did not state so. The difficulty was that the friends inflated their imaginations beyond reason; and that when their imaginations burst asunder, they were inclined to throw away everything" (232).

One Web site notes the changes in Watchtower date setting that began to take place during the Rutherford years following the disappointment of 1925. Some of these dates involve earlier years, which we have not discussed but which indicate the early Watchtower fondness for predicting end-time events:

> From 1925 to 1933, their eschatological [end-time] beliefs underwent radical changes. By 1933, 1914 was seen as the beginning of Christ's presence, his enthronement as king and the start of the last days instead of being considered the terminal date for chronology. The 1878 resurrection date was changed to 1918 and the teaching of the judgment of religious groups was moved to 1919. These are the current teachings of Jehovah's Witnesses regarding 1914, 1918 and 1919. They no longer consider the dates 1799, 1874 and 1878 to have any eschatological significance. (Answers.com, "History," July 3, 2006, 6)

In spite of the 1925 failure, the hope of the return of the patriarchs remained. The Watchtower subsequently purchased land and built a mansion in San Diego, as a place where the returned Old Testament greats could stay. The place was called Beth-Sarim, Hebrew for "House of Princes." In the deed, Rutherford put the house "in perpetual trust for the ancient kings and prophets of Palestine" (Gruss and Chretein, "Beth-Sarim" 25).

The March 15, 1937, *Watchtower* said, "The press has scoffed at Beth-Sarim, but those faithful men of old will be back before Armageddon ends" (86). In 1942, the year of Rutherford's death, the prediction was that the "faithful men of old may be expected back from the dead any day now" (28).

Nevertheless, in 1948, the organization sold the property. Later publications adjusted the prophecy:

> At the time [Beth-Sarim was being used by the Society], it was believed that faithful men of old

times, such as Abraham, Joseph, and David, would be resurrected before the end of this system of things and would serve as "princes in all the earth," in fulfillment of Psalm 45:16. This view was adjusted in 1950, when further study of the Scriptures indicated that those earthly forefathers of Jesus Christ would be resurrected after Armageddon. (*Jehovah's Witnesses: Proclaimers of God's Kingdom* 76)

The *1975 Yearbook* of the organization simply said that Beth-Sarim had been built for "Brother" Rutherford's use (Reed, *Index* 63).

1975: The Year of Christ's Return

The statement about Beth-Sarim having been built for Judge Rutherford's use was not entirely false. It was a mansion, and he lived a life of comfort there. But it was also a life increasingly given over to drink, especially following the failure of the 1925 prophecies (Gruss and Chretein, "Beth-Sarim" 27). Mentioning Rutherford's personal life, which by insiders and outsiders alike has been acknowledged as controversial, is significant, not only because it underscores the human vulnerability of Watchtower leadership but also because it calls attention to the immense psychological strain that the organization's constant state of expectation and deflation has had upon people, from the top down. This is a point we will return to in chapter 10.

Each of the first two leaders of the Society, then, was deeply involved in prophecies; and each was shown to be a false prophet concerning a major prediction. Following the 1925 failure, many left the organization (Gruss and Chretein, "Beth-Sarim" 27).

At times there were indications that the organization had learned its lesson, as in the 1931 Watchtower publication *Vindication:* "There was a measure of disappointment on the part of Jehovah's faithful ones on earth concerning the years

When do 6,000 Years End?

How can it be determined when 6,000 years of human history will end? According to reliable Bible chronology, Adam and Eve were created in 4026 B.C.E..* From the autumn of

4026 B.C.E. to 1 B.C.E.	4,025 years
1 B.C.E. to 1 C.E.	1 year
1 C.E. to 1968 C.E.	1,967 years
Total to autumn 1968	5,993 years

This would leave only seven more years from the autumn of 1968 to complete 6,000 full years of human history. That seven-year period will evidently finish in the autumn of the year 1975.

END OF WORLD IN 1914

NOT THE VIEW OF PASTOR RUSSELL NOR OF I. B. S. A.

Watchtower prophecies

1917, 1918, and 1925, which disappointment lasted for a time . . . and they also learned to quit fixing dates" (338, quoted on Christian Apologetics and Research Ministry Web site). The references to 1917 and 1918 relate to the Society's predictions concerning "the destruction of Christendom in 1914 to 1918 A.D." (*Studies in the Scriptures,* Vol. 7, 398, quoted in Reed, *Index* 103). In spite of such failed prophecies, the Society was not yet ready to stop setting dates. The organization's third president, Nathan H. Knorr, would be involved in another major prophetic debacle, this one involving the year 1975.

This time the prophecy was less direct and more subtle, but suggestive just the same. The May 1, 1967, *Watchtower* suggested, ". . . 1975 marks the end of 6,000 years of human experiences. . . . Will it be the time when God executes the wicked? . . . It very well could be, but we will have to wait and see" (262). Under the heading "Why are you looking forward to 1975?" an article in the August 15, 1968, issue of the *Watchtower* raised expectations:

> What about all this talk concerning the year 1975? Lively discussions, some based on speculation, have burst into flame during recent months among serious students of the Bible. Their interest has been kindled by the belief that 1975 will mark the end of 6,000 years of human history since Adam's creation. The nearness of such an important date

115

indeed fires the imagination and presents unlimited possibilities for discussion. (494)

As the date drew nearer, Witnesses were told not to pursue higher education because there was so very little time left (*Watchtower,* March 15, 1969, 171), and since there was such a short time left, Witnesses were told to study no longer than six months with a prospective convert (*Watchtower,* May 15, 1969, 312).

The growing sense of urgency greatly affected the personal lives of many Witnesses. "Reports are heard of brothers selling their homes and property and planning to finish out the rest of their days in this old system in the pioneer service. Certainly this is a fine way to spend the short time remaining before the wicked world's end" (*Our Kingdom Ministry* monthly, May 1974, 3, quoted in Reed, *Index* 109). "A great crowd of people are confident that great destruction is imminent, which has been a major factor in their decision not to have children" (*Awake!* November 8, 1974, 11).

After all was said and done, 1975 came and went without the anticipated destructions. When nothing happened, the July 15, 1976, *Watchtower* declared:

> But it is not advisable for us to set our sights on a certain date. . . . If anyone has been disappointed through not following this line of thought, he should now concentrate on adjusting his viewpoint, seeing that it was not the word of God that failed or deceived him and brought disappointment, but that his own understanding was based on wrong premises. (441)

Once again blaming the poor followers, Jehovah's Witness president Frederick W. Franz told a large gathering of Witnesses that the reason "why nothing happened in 1975 [was] because *you* expected something to happen" (Bowman, "The Whitewashing of the Watchtower" 12).

The Legacy of Failed Prophecies

A true prophet of God does not err in foretelling the future. A false prophet does. The Jehovah's Witness organization, which claims to be God's prophet, has shown itself to be a false prophet. Even by its own standards, the Watchtower organization is condemned. According to an article in *Awake!* magazine (October 8, 1968), "There have been those in times past who predicted an 'end to the world,' even announcing a specific date. . . . The end did not come. They were guilty of false prophesying. Why? What was missing? Missing from such people were God's truths and evidence that he was using and guiding them" (Magnani 73).

More important, by the inerrant standard of God's Word, the Holy Scriptures, the Society stands condemned. Jesus warned, "At that time if anyone says to you, 'Look, here is the Christ!' or, 'There he is!' do not believe it. For false Christs and false prophets will appear and perform great signs and miracles to deceive even the elect—if that were possible. See, I have told you ahead of time" (Matthew 24:23-25).

Having been exposed in the glaring light of truth, the Watchtower organization has had to deal with its failed prophecies. It has done so in several ways—ignoring the failed prophecies, changing them to mean something different, or making light of them.

The Watchtower's official history, *Jehovah's Witnesses: Proclaimers of God's Kingdom,* provides an example of the last method. There we read of how as the awaited date of Christ's return in October 1914 approached, one key Watchtower leader, A. H. Macmillan (a confidant to the first three Watchtower presidents), told a group in Sarasota Springs, New York, "This is probably the last public address I shall ever deliver because we shall be going home [to heaven] soon."

A couple of days later, Macmillan "came in for some good-natured teasing" as, in his own words, "everybody laughed heartily" about his earlier remarks. "I tried to show

117

the friends that perhaps some of us had been a bit too hasty in thinking that we were going to heaven right away, and the thing for us to do would be to keep busy in the Lord's service until he determined when any of his approved servants would be taken home to heaven" (62).

The reason some members had been "too hasty" was that they were being misled by an organization led by a false prophet. The Society recovered quickly and, so the history explains, "the Bible Students were not 'taken home' to heaven in October 1914. Nevertheless, the Gentile Times did end in that year. Clearly, the Bible Students had more to learn as to the significance of 1914. Meanwhile, what were they to do? Work!" (*Jehovah's Witnesses: Proclaimers* 62-3)

When confronted with prophecies from Watchtower literature, Jehovah's Witnesses might toss out the argument that they are taken out of context or offer the excuse that the writers didn't claim to be the prophet of God. Neither answer holds any water.

Today Jehovah's Witnesses seem more ready to admit that the organization's leadership made mistakes in its predictions and that it was not simply a matter of individual members misinterpreting the literature (Kern 48). Some Witnesses will admit the mistake and argue that the organization is becoming wiser with age. In a personal interview with a Jehovah's Witness, I was somewhat surprised how easily this individual spoke of the organization's previous "false prophecies," using the term several times and brushing them off as the kind of mistakes any organization might make as it develops and improves itself.

Yet the facts remain that the prophecies come right out of the Witnesses' literature; true prophets do not make mistakes (Deuteronomy 18:22); Jesus says we should beware of false prophets (Matthew 7:15). How can people rely on an organization that is a proven false prophet? How can they trust what they are taught now by the Watchtower? Will that also change to fit the later needs of the Society's leaders?

118

Part 3.
The Christian Witness to Witnesses

9. The Way of Salvation

Since the Scriptures clearly say that the 144,000 are the only ones besides Christ Jesus that have part in the heavenly resurrection, does this not argue that there will be no others that will come forth from the tomb? No; there will be an earthly resurrection. The greater mass of humankind will find life here on earth amid paradise conditions. (*Let God Be True* 276)

In the previous chapter, we examined some of the Watchtower's erroneous end-time predictions. As important as the matter of dates and predictions regarding Christ's return might be, even more vital is how Jehovah's Witnesses approach the question that the jailer in Philippi asked of Paul and Silas, "Sirs, what must I do to be saved?" (Acts 16:30). While Jehovah's Witnesses speak of the ransom that Jesus made, they point to good works as the way to heaven, or paradise. Moreover, they believe that only 144,000 will go to heaven and the rest of the believers will live in a paradise on earth.

Salvation Is a Gift

"For God so loved the world that he gave his one and only Son, that whoever believes in him shall not perish but have eternal life" (John 3:16).

"For it is by grace you have been saved, through faith— and this not from yourselves, it is the gift of God—not by works, so that no one can boast" (Ephesians 2:8,9).

Faith and Good Works

When it comes to the eternal salvation of souls, the Bible is unmistakable: "By grace you have been saved, through faith—and this not from yourselves, it is the gift of God—not by works, so that no one can boast" (Ephesians 2:8,9). Nevertheless, for Jehovah's Witnesses, faith is not enough. In addition, they must, in the words of a former Witness, "work, work, work" (Hewitt 124). Witnesses see good works as necessary for salvation. Indeed, the Watchtower has set up four requirements:

> Jesus Christ identified a first requirement when he said in prayer to his Father: "This means everlasting life, their *taking in knowledge* of you, the only true God, and of the one whom you sent forth, Jesus Christ." (John 17:3) Knowledge of God

and of Jesus Christ includes knowledge of God's purposes. . . .

Many have found the second requirement more difficult. It is to *obey God's laws*, yes, to conform one's life to the moral requirements set out in the Bible. This includes refraining from a debauched, immoral way of life.—1 Corinthians 6:9,10; 1 Peter 4:3,4.

A third requirement is that we *be associated with God's channel*, his organization. . . . To receive everlasting life in the earthly Paradise we must identify that organization and serve God as part of it.

The fourth requirement is connected with loyalty. God requires that prospective subjects of his Kingdom support his government by *loyally advocating his Kingdom rule to others*. . . . (*Watchtower,* February 15, 1983, 12-13, italics in original)

Numerous other statements endorse this. The September 15, 1989, *Watchtower* says, "Yes, there are various things involved in getting saved. We must take in accurate knowledge of God's purposes and his way of salvation. Then we must exercise faith in the Chief Agent of salvation, Jesus Christ, and do God's will the rest of our lives. (John 3:16; Titus 2:14)" (7). The book *You Can Live Forever in Paradise on Earth* states, "However, more than faith is needed. There must also be works to demonstrate what your true feelings are about Jehovah" (250). Salvation, then, depends on human achievement, on making oneself worthy: "Those who stay loyal to God will be judged worthy of everlasting life" (*The Truth That Leads to Eternal Life* 113).

The Witness system of works emphasizes what is done for the organization. Door-to-door witnessing, notes Herbert Kern, is "one of the most important requirements" for

Witnesses' salvation (7). A *Watchtower* article, "Baptism—A Christian Requirement" underscores this: "It is evident . . . that besides faith and baptism, 'public declaration' to the effect that Jesus Christ is Lord and that God raised him up from the dead is a requirement for salvation" (May 1, 1979, 15). Rather than being seen as a means of grace through which we enjoy "the washing of rebirth and renewal by the Holy Spirit" (Titus 3:5), baptism, like door-to-door witnessing, becomes but another requirement, a view that tragically some Christians share.

At the risk of belaboring our point, one last quotation from the *Watchtower* will drive home the Society's oppressive obsession with salvation by works:

> When a person, on the basis of the Scriptural knowledge he has gained, has belief it would be a mistake for him [one who has belief in Christ] to think that he is now saved and cannot fall. He must show by his endurance in the Christian faith that he is worthy of salvation. . . . Salvation from death is a gift from God to those that obey him, not to those that disobey. (March 1, 1960, 134)

Instead of the Bible's exhortations to do good works being taken as opportunities to respond to God's love in Jesus Christ, they become demands and burdens that must be borne to get into heaven. A statement from *Let God Be True* sums it up: "Christ Jesus received immortality as a reward for his faithful course of action, and it is also given, as a reward, to those who are of the true church or 'body of Christ'. Immortality is a reward for faithfulness" (65-6).

The Jehovah's Witness emphasis on good works brings to mind Paul's stern words to the Galatians: "You foolish Galatians! Who has bewitched you? Before your very eyes Jesus Christ was clearly portrayed as crucified. . . . Did you receive the Spirit by observing the law, or by believing what you heard? Are you so foolish? After beginning with the Spirit, are you now trying to attain your goal by human effort?" (3:1-3). Sadly, whereas the Galatians had fallen away from the truth into a religion of works, many Jehovah's Witnesses have lived their entire lives under the slavery of works. Don Luke comments on his days as a Jehovah's Witness:

> I never felt like I was doing enough for the church. The talks focus on "Are you truly doing all you can?" . . . In addition, the terminology used to communicate and underscore Jehovah's Witnesses [teaching] is a key point. What a Jehovah's Witness means by "Christ is my Savior" and "Christ's role" is very different from how most Christians would understand. (e-mail to author)

Although Witnesses speak of Jesus as Savior, the emphasis and attention in the Jehovah's Witness system is clearly on works. Referring to this emphasis as the "torture of being a Jehovah's Witness," Amy Mueller adds, "There are never enough good works. [Witnesses] have law without gospel. The burden of guilt from our shortcomings is never alleviated by grace" (e-mail to author).

All of this is quite different from the answer that Paul and Silas gave to that jailer long ago who asked how he could be saved: "They replied, 'Believe in the Lord Jesus, and you will be saved—you and your household'" (Acts 16:31). Jehovah's Witnesses are bothered when someone *knows* he or she is going to heaven (Hewitt 113). Yet we can and do know, for through the Scriptures the Holy Spirit has planted faith in our hearts so that we know and believe that when Jesus died for the sins of the world that included ours.

The Life to Come

As for the condition of those who are saved and those who are lost, once again the Society teaches contrary to the Scriptures. It denies the existence of hell and divides the saved into two classes, who will live in two different places.

Annihilation

According to Watchtower theology, those who are lost will not go to hell. Rather, Jehovah's Witnesses believe that people who do not accept their message will be annihilated (Kern 50). This springs from the notion that the soul and body are inseparable and that the "human soul dies" and is "not immortal" (*Make Sure of All Things* 263).

In the Jehovah's Witnesses scheme of things, the word *soul* is just another word for "life," and once a person dies, the soul ceases to exist. Once more taking aim at the theologians and Bible scholars, the organization states, ". . . you can look at Genesis 1:20,30 and note that fish, birds, and animals are in the 'living creature' class . . . men and beasts are *souls* . . . Thus we see that the claim of religionists that man has an immortal soul, and therefore differs from the beast, is not Scriptural" (*Let God Be True* 59-60).

Citing Ecclesiastes 3:19,20, *Let God Be True* goes on to point out that "all [men and beasts] turn to dust again" (67). Further on in Ecclesiastes, the text states that death is a time when "the dust returns to the ground it came from, and the spirit returns to God who gave it" (12:7). The Witness tract "Do You Have an Immortal Spirit?" contends this passage means that "once that force [the spirit] is gone from a person, only God has the ability to restore it to him. So the spirit 'returns to the true God' in that any hope of future life for that person now rests entirely with God" (4-5). This sounds fine, except that if a person completely ceases to exist, then to talk of a return (or any action) makes no sense. How can something that does not exist do anything?

When man fell into sin, the Lord declared that he would return to dust (Genesis 3:19), yet the spirit that God breathed into him (Genesis 2:7) would return to God to be judged. Thus the soul separates from the body at the time a person dies. Indeed, death always denotes a separation. The soul separates from the body at the time of physical death. The sinner is separated from God and spiritually dead until brought to faith in Christ, as Paul noted to the Ephesian Christians, "As for you, you were dead in your transgressions and sins, in which you used to live" (Ephesians 2:1,2). Eternal death marks everlasting separation from God. So, while it is true that both men and beasts return to the dust, this does not mean that a person is annihilated.

There are many Bible passages that speak of torment for the damned. Yet, according to Witness theology: "The doctrine of a burning hell where the wicked are tormented eternally after death cannot be true, mainly for four reasons: (1) Because it is wholly unscriptural; (2) because it is unreasonable; (3) because it is contrary to God's love; and (4) because it is repugnant to justice" (*Let God Be True* 80). Witnesses refer to hell as "this God-dishonoring doctrine" of which the "promulgator . . . is Satan himself" (*Let God Be True* 79).

Scripture says otherwise. Indeed, "God is love" (1 John 4:8,16), but he is also just. Jesus, who in love came to die for the sins of the world, warns about "the fire of hell" (Matthew 5:22) and speaks of those who "will go away to eternal punishment" (Matthew 25:46). Hell, according to Jesus, is not a condition of being annihilated but a place "where there will be weeping and gnashing of teeth" (Matthew 25:30).

Erstwhile Jehovah's Witness Joe Hewitt points to the seriousness of the organization's error, "The Watchtower's hell-denying doctrine is a narcotic to numb the minds of people headed there, so they won't repent and believe the gospel" (106).

Heaven and Paradise on Earth

As for those who are saved, the Watchtower organization teaches there are two places for them—heaven and paradise on earth. Only 144,000 people will go to heaven: "The Bible says that only 144,000 will go to heaven to be with Christ. Have you never read that in the Bible? . . . It is here at Revelation 14:1,3" (*Reasoning from the Scriptures* 361, also

125

166-7). This is the "little flock" that for a thousand years will "reign" with Christ in theocratic rule over the angels and the faithful people here on earth (*Let God Be True* 121-4). In drawing upon the book of Revelation, Witnesses argue that the 12 tribes of Israel spoken of there are not literally Israelites, but that the number 144,000 is to be taken literally.

Only the 144,000 Witnesses "who are heirs with [Jesus] of the heavenly Kingdom" are born again (*Reasoning from the Scriptures* 76). Arguing that flesh and blood cannot enter heaven, Witnesses believe that these people "expect to be born like Jesus Christ into the fullness of spirit life in heaven, changed, transformed indeed" (*Your Will Be Done on Earth* 50).

Also known as the Anointed Class, the Bride of Christ, and the Faithful and Discreet Slave, these are the handful who partake of the bread and wine in the Society's annual Memorial, the mandatory yearly observance of the Lord's Evening Meal, which is sometimes compared to Communion in many churches. Others in attendance simply observe, although everyone takes part in passing the bread and wine around.

Only the anointed Witnesses receive other special benefits, including the benefit of Jesus' mediation on their behalf: "Likewise, the Greater Moses, Jesus Christ, is not the Mediator between Jehovah God and all mankind. He is the Mediator between his heavenly Father, Jehovah God, and the nation of spiritual Israel, which is limited to only 144,000 members" (*The Desire for Peace and Security Worldwide* 10, quoted in Christian Apologetics and Research Ministry).

The gathering of this elite group began with the apostles and, according to Judge Rutherford, was completed by the year 1935 (Rhodes, *Reasoning from the Scriptures* 254). This consisted of people who were age 10 or older at the time of Christ's invisible return in 1914. For years it was taught that members of the generation of the 144,000 would be alive at the time of Armageddon, that is, the great battle that will usher in the millennium. An *Awake!* article asserted that of "the generation alive in 1914, some will see the major fulfillment of Christ Jesus' prophecy and the destruction" (October 8, 1973, 19). A *Watchtower* article added, "Before the 1914 generation completely dies out, God's judgment must be executed" (May 1, 1985, 4).

With the passing years, the number of this elite group has dwindled to almost nothing, yet the cataclysmic events they were to witness have not yet transpired. As is the case with so many other Witness teachings, the nature of the 144,000 is also changing. Don Luke notes:

> One interesting observation I have made is how Jehovah's Witnesses are changing who makes up the governing body. When I was young, the Governing Body was only part of the 144,000. That group had also been born to witness the signs of the last days, starting in 1914. Since anyone that age now is very, very old, I am wondering how the Jehovah's Witnesses changed that belief. I think that they now allow members of the great crowd [other Witnesses] or maybe members of the 144,000 who haven't been around since 1914. (e-mail to author)

Indeed, the Watchtower must make adjustments rapidly as another of its predictions comes to naught.

In addition to the special 144,000, other Jehovah's Witnesses are known as the "other sheep" or the "great crowd." This multitude of people is faithful to Jehovah but is not selected for heavenly life. There is no fixed number for this group, which continues to bring more into the fold. They will survive Armageddon and live in the "new system" or paradise established on earth. *Let God Be True* offers a description of the renewed earth:

127

> In the purified earth, free from evil Satanic
> influence, and with the sin-canceling merit of
> Christ's sacrifice operating toward them, the sur-
> vivors of Armageddon, under the direction of the
> King and his princes, will marry and bring forth
> children in righteousness. . . . Every child, reared
> in the "nurture and admonition of the Lord", will
> have full opportunity for life through Christ the
> King; any not desiring to serve Jehovah shall
> perish, rightly . . . (265)

With such "clever human reasoning that panders to human
emotions," says Amy Mueller, Jehovah's Witnesses "explain
away all the troubling questions about Judgment Day,
unbaptized children, unbelievers who never heard the gospel,
etc. They do not allow God to be God" (e-mail to author).

During the thousand years of paradise on earth, Satan will
be "imprisoned" and billions of the "unjust" dead will be
raised to be instructed in God's law (*Let God Be True* 266).
Toward the end of the millennium, Satan will be unleashed,
only to be vanquished once and for all along with those who
side with him. After that will come the "wicked-less" world
without end. Non-Witnesses are invited to become members
of the great crowd: "Would you enjoy living in it? If yes, then
become one of the 'other sheep' now, share in the heart-cheering
proclamation of the Kingdom, and be assured of God's blessing,
guidance and protection, as your steps lead you into full
realization of the glorious life-prospect ahead" (*Let God Be
True* 266-7).

In the Bible, the new heaven and new earth are not two
distinct places, any more than the little flock and great multitude are two distinct classes. They are different ways of
portraying the glories ahead for the saved, who in relation to
the many who perish are a little flock but who still constitute
a great multitude.

In the book of Revelation, John describes a great crowd or multitude in heaven: "After this I looked and there before me was a great multitude that no one could count, from every nation, tribe, people and language, standing before the throne and in front of the Lamb" (7:9). As might be expected, Witnesses have an answer: "The description of them as 'standing before the throne and before the Lamb' indicates not necessarily a location, but an approved condition. . . . The expression 'before the throne' . . . does not require that they be in heaven" (*Reasoning from the Scriptures* 167). When the term is used in Revelation 19:1,6, Witnesses contend that it refers not to people but to angels (*Reasoning from the Scriptures* 168). The pattern of trying to force the Scriptures to square with Watchtower doctrine is evident.

One of the most striking examples of this is Luke 23:43, where Jesus said to the criminal on the cross next to him, "I tell you the truth, today you will be with me in paradise." Since Witnesses believe that the soul does not live on when the body dies, Jesus could not have meant what he said. The *New World Translation* has "Truly I tell you today, you will be with me in Paradise." By shifting the comma, the Watchtower has changed the meaning. The Greek text does not have commas, yet the meaning is clear. Similar to the Old Testament expression "Thus says the LORD," the phrase "I tell you the truth" is a standard way of introducing key statements in the New Testament. Of the 74 times the New Testament uses the expression, the *New World Translation* places a break immediately after it 73 times, with Luke 23:43 the sole exception.

In response to the criminal's request that Jesus remember him when Jesus entered his kingdom, Christ reassured him that he would be in paradise that very day. There is still more to this text, as Robert Bowman points out:

> Jesus promised the thief: "You will be *with me* in Paradise" [emphasis his]. This contradicts the JW's doctrine in two ways. First, "you will be with me"

implies that all believers in Christ will live in His presence, whereas JWs think that most believers—including the thief in question—will live on the earth while a select few will live in heaven with Christ. Second, "with me in Paradise" implies that Christ went to paradise, whereas JWs think that Paradise will be on earth and Christ will stay in heaven. ("Jehovah's Witnesses and Luke 23:43" 4)

Every word of Scripture is filled with assurance and with truth. How tragic that the Watchtower organization robs people of the comfort of salvation and twists Scripture to fit its false notions of the life to come and salvation!

As with the end times (eschatology), so in regard to salvation (soteriology), the Watchtower has misled its people. What a treasure it is to know the simple gospel, the good news, that Christ has done everything necessary for our salvation. He has lived the perfect life in our stead, laid down that life as a sacrifice for the sins of the world, and risen again to open the gates of heaven. "He was delivered over to death for our sins and was raised to life for our justification" (Romans 4:25).

The times we live in are evil, and every indication is that we are living in the last days. The penultimate verse of the Bible's last book says, "He [Jesus] who testifies to these things says, 'Yes, I am coming soon.'" To which believers respond, "Amen. Come, Lord Jesus" (Revelation 22:20). The precise time of that coming is in God's hands. What time we do have here on earth, we can use in service to God and our fellow human beings. We do so not in a frantic effort to earn salvation but in response to the salvation Christ has earned. That life of service includes reaching out to others, including Jehovah's Witnesses, with the love of Jesus Christ.

10. Christian Freedom Versus Legalism

One by one, all holiday celebrations were eliminated from my life. A sense of self-righteousness replaced the sense of loss; a feeling of pride welled up within me, as I comforted myself that I was more pleasing to Jehovah than were people of the world who were still relishing in their pagan celebrations.

Christmas was the one holiday I mourned losing. Beloved carols I had sung all my life wafted through the air at shopping malls during Christmastime; often I found myself unconsciously humming along with the strains of cherished melodies. When I became aware of what I was doing, I felt so guilty that I found it necessary to avoid the malls altogether during that time of year to avoid sinning against Jehovah. (Diane Wilson, *Awakening of a Jehovah's Witness* 31)

One of the priceless treasures that we enjoy as Christians is freedom from man-made laws. The apostle Paul wrote, "It is for freedom that Christ has set us free. Stand firm, then, and do not let yourselves be burdened again by a yoke of slavery" (Galatians 5:1). The early Christians had to struggle against the notion that they were still bound by the ceremonial laws of the Old Testament or that somehow the keeping of various rites would help earn their salvation.

Legalism, the tendency to live under laws, comes easily to people, for it is the natural religion of sinful human beings to think that we must (and can) somehow earn our own way into heaven. For Jehovah's Witnesses, legalism is a way of life. Back in 1980, a Watchtower vice-president said, "When we talk about law, we talk about organization. With all our hearts we need to search after that law. Jehovah doesn't give individuals interpretation [of the Scriptures]. We need a guide, and that is the *'faithful and discreet slave'*" (quoted in Penton 122).

Not only does the Society control the interpretation of Scripture, it also lays on its members the heavy burden of legalism. This is evident in the many man-made laws that bind the consciences of Witnesses, when they should be free to decide how to live their own lives. This chapter discusses a number of issues—from the shape of Jesus' cross to the celebration of holidays—that give evidence to Witness legalism.

Christians and Legalism

"It is for freedom that Christ has set us free. Stand firm, then, and do not let yourselves be burdened again by a yoke of slavery" (Galatians 5:1).

Martin Luther: "People make a Moses [lawgiver] of Christ for us, whereas he did not purchase us with His shed blood merely to teach us how to live a good life, but in order to live and rule in us Himself and to be our Lord, working all good works within us, something that takes place only through faith in Him" (*What Luther Says,* I:539 185).

The Cross of Christ

In the New Testament accounts of the death of Jesus, the *New World Translation* translates the Greek word *stauros* as "torture stake" rather than "cross." Jehovah's Witnesses argue that the word *stauros* meant "upright stake," rather than the traditional cross with a horizontal bar. Thus, for example, John 19:17 reads, "And, bearing the torture stake for himself, he [Jesus] went out to the so-called Skull Place, which is called Golgotha in Hebrew."

"Crux simplex," a simple wooden torture stake

At first glance the argument may seem trivial. Most people react—as did a group of students I had who heard a presentation by a Jehovah's Witness on the subject—by saying, "What difference does it make? What matters is that Jesus died for our sins." The Society's insistence on this point, however, is not just about the shape of the instrument of Jesus' death. It is part of an overall attempt to prove that Christianity and its symbols are based not on biblical truths but on pagan, pre-Christian practices and falsehoods.

The Witness argument is that the cross was actually a symbol used in pre-Christian times and is a representation of false gods, such as Bel from ancient Chaldea or the Greek (actually Roman) Bacchus: "So by cherishing the cross, a person is honoring a symbol of worship that is opposed to the true God" (*Reasoning from the Scriptures* 92). As far as Witnesses are concerned, the cross is a pagan symbol and should be avoided. Witnesses consider stepping inside a church and seeing a cross equivalent to entering a place that is under the control of the devil.

As is the case for many of the Society's arguments, this one is based on half-truths. Indeed, the word *stauros* can mean stake. Yet, as the *Eerdmans Bible Dictionary* points out, "Originally merely a stake on which the victim was tied or impaled, by Roman times the cross featured a horizontal beam, placed either on top of the vertical shaft . . . or slightly below the top" (246). Ron Rhodes adds:

> The Jehovah's Witnesses fail to point out that the Greek word *stauros* was used to refer to a variety of wooden structures used for execution in ancient days. Robert Bowman notes that *stauros* as a wooden structure could represent shapes similar to the Greek letter *tau* (T) and the plus sign (+), occasionally using two diagonal beams (X), as well as (infrequently) a simple upright stake with no crosspiece. To argue that only the last-named

form was used, or that *stauros* could be used only for that form, is contradictory to the actual historical facts and is based on a naive restriction of the term to its original or simplest meaning. ("Crucifixion by Cross")

The biblical text supports the traditional understanding. Even in the *New World Translation,* John 20:25 reads, "Consequently the other disciples would say to him: 'We have seen the Lord!' But he [Thomas] said to them: 'Unless I see in his hands the print of the nails and stick my finger into the print of the nails and stick my hand into his side, I will certainly not believe.'" If Jesus had been nailed to a stake, only one nail would have been used to go through both of his hands, as Jehovah's Witness publications picture it (*You Can Live Forever in Paradise on Earth* 170). Yet the Bible says that nails (plural) were used—one for each outstretched hand.

Moreover, in another related and significant detail, Scripture speaks of the sign ordered by the Roman Governor Pontius Pilate being placed "above his [Jesus'] head" (Matthew 27:37), not his hands, as he hung on the cross.

When Jesus spoke to Peter of his (Peter's) future crucifixion, he indirectly alluded to the traditional cross. Jesus said to him, "'I tell you the truth, . . . when you are old you will stretch out your hands. . . .' Jesus said this to indicate the kind of death by which Peter would glorify God" (John 21:18,19). According to tradition, Peter was crucified upside down on an inverted cross.

As if to underscore the arbitrary nature of Witness arguments concerning the cross, early editions of the *Watchtower* magazine carried the cross on the cover. The 1921 publication *The Harp of God* makes no mention of the torture stake but makes frequent mention of the cross of Christ and has an uncritical illustration of Jesus on a traditional cross.

Christians should continue to display the cross and honor it as the correct symbol of our Savior's sacrificial death for our sins. With the writer of the beautiful Lenten hymn, we can declare, "In the cross of Christ I glory" (quoted approvingly in *The Harp of God* 143), or in the words of the apostle Paul, "May I never boast except in the cross of our Lord Jesus Christ" (Galatians 6:14).

Blood Transfusions

The Old Testament forbad to God's chosen people the pagan practice of eating blood (Leviticus 17:10), a principle that was reiterated in the New Testament at the Council at Jerusalem (Acts 15:29). Since the mid-1940s (Penton 153), Jehovah's Witnesses have considered blood transfusions a form of eating blood:

> In a hospital, when a patient cannot eat through his mouth, he is fed intravenously. Now, would a person who never put blood into his mouth but who accepted blood by transfusion really be obeying the command to "keep abstaining from . . . blood"? (Acts 15:29) To use a comparison, consider a man who is told by the doctor that he must abstain from alcohol. Would he be obedient if he quit drinking alcohol but had it put directly into his veins? (*Reasoning from the Scriptures* 73)

Over the years the Watchtower position on blood transfusions has been inconsistent; Diane Wilson devotes a lengthy chapter, "Playing Follow-the-Leader: Zigzagging Doctrines that Affect Lives," to documenting numerous changes in doctrines, especially in regard to medical questions (167-216). The current position makes distinctions among different types of transfusions; although whole blood transfusions are rejected, derivatives of blood are not (Kern 53-4). An Internet article summarizes:

> In current medical practice, whole blood transfusions are very rare, and blood derivatives are used instead.

Witnesses may accept a process called normovolemic hemodilution, a treatment that processes the individual's own blood in a closed loop that does not interrupt the circulation of blood, and delivers it immediately back into the person's body. . . . Many members carry carefully prepared durable power of attorney documentation outlining their medical wishes with respect to blood. (*Wikipedia*, "Beliefs and Practices," June 21, 2006, 7)

While calling attention to potential dangers of blood transfusions (for example, being infected with AIDS), Witnesses state that they "have no religious objection to the use of nonblood [sic] plasma expanders" (*Reasoning from the Scriptures* 73).

Nevertheless, despite attempts to play down the harshness of their position, the fact remains that they will choose death for themselves and their children rather than break what they consider to be God's law. The 1961 Watchtower publication *Blood, Medicine and the Law of God* is emphatic: "They [Witnesses] know that if they violate God's law and the child dies in the process, they have endangered that child's opportunity for everlasting life in God's new world. . . . It may result in the immediate and very temporary prolongation of life, but at the cost of eternal life for a dedicated Christian" (quoted in Reed, *Index of Watchtower Errors* 69).

Don Luke explains the seriousness of this Watchtower rule:

Accepting a blood transfusion is considered a sin more serious than theft or adultery. Thieves and adulterers are more quickly forgiven by Watchtower judicial committees than individuals found guilty of taking blood. A Witness must refuse blood in all circumstances, even when this is certain to result in death. The organization also requires adults to refuse transfusions for their minor children. (e-mail to author)

137

The Watchtower's "absurdly literal" (Grizzuti Harrison 98) reading of the passages that forbid eating animal blood—but not human blood transfusions—has led to countless tragedies. The cover of the May 22, 1994, *Awake!* magazine featured the photographs of 26 children who, according to the caption, were "Youths who put God first." In other words, they died in keeping with the Watchtower injunction against blood transfusions, which could save children suffering from diseases such as leukemia.

Birthdays

"Jehovah's Witnesses do not share in birthday festivities" because they "tend to give excessive importance to an individual" (*School and Jehovah's Witnesses* 18, quoted in Kern 54). "Celebrating a birthday in any manner is strictly forbidden," writes Don Luke. "Even sending a birthday card can bring action against the offender by an official judicial committee. The punishment is (may be) disfellowshiping." (Despite the Society's injunctions against birthdays, one Jehovah's Witness did admit to me the modest celebration of birthdays in her household.)

The Bible has two specific references to birthday celebrations. One is the birthday of the Egyptian pharaoh, which led to the release of his cupbearer from prison and the beheading of the chief baker (Genesis 40:20-22), and the other is the infamous birthday of King Herod, which led to the beheading of John the Baptist (Matthew 14:1-12). Since both involved wicked pagans and pronouncements of death, it is reasoned that Christians should avoid birthday celebrations.

That is an argument from silence or guilt by association (the celebration is evil because there are one or two examples of bad people holding birthday celebrations). Yet the Bible never explicitly condemns birthdays. In a positive way, Job 1:4 refers to the sons of Job holding feasts in their house, literally, "each one on his day," most likely a reference to birthday celebrations. Christian families will use birthday celebrations as an opportunity to thank God for the gift of life for the celebrant and for the opportunity of a life of service to the Savior.

The Celebration of Holidays

The Jehovah's Witness opposition to the celebration of Christmas is well known. But that is not the only holiday that is off limits for Witnesses. Easter and others are forbidden as well.

Christmas

The Bible does not state the date of Jesus' birth, but there are reasons behind the belief that Jesus' birth may have been on or about December 25. The church father Hippolytus (about 170–235) is credited as the first person to settle on the date of December 25 (Ehlke 340). He concluded that the time of Christ's life from his conception to his crucifixion was exactly 33 years. Having determined that both these events took place on March 25, it was simply a matter of adding nine months to arrive at the date of December 25 for Jesus' birthday.

In the pagan Roman Empire, December 25 marked the annual Saturnalia, associated with the god Saturn and coinciding with the celebration of the winter solstice. It has often been suggested that as Christianity gained in influence and eventually became legitimate, Christians replaced the Saturnalia with the celebration of the Savior's birth. This may well be the case. Throughout the succeeding centuries, Christians have had the challenge of keeping the focus on Christ in Christmas.

Following this line of thinking and noting parallels such as the exchange of gifts and other practices associated with both the Saturnalia and Christmas, an *Awake!* article expressed the Watchtower position that Christmas is "a celebration that is neither commanded nor mentioned in Scripture, but that was borrowed from . . . pagan celebrations" (December 8, 1961, 8, quoted in Hoekema 237). Taking the position that the shepherds would not have been outside in the winter, Witnesses contend, "Jesus was not born on

December 25th . . . Hence, celebrating his birthday through Christmas observance on December 25 is totally inappropriate for those guided by the Holy Scriptures" (*Watchtower*, December 15, 1979, 5). According to the *Watchtower*, the source of "Christmas and its music" is not Jehovah, but "Satan the Devil" (December 15, 1983, 7).

Although the celebration of Christmas is forbidden among Witnesses, it was not always that way. Early editions of the *Watchtower* commended the practice, even suggesting giving the *Studies in Scriptures* for Christmas gifts. (See Reed, *Index of Watchtower Errors* 72.)

If some Christians choose not to celebrate their Savior's birth on December 25, they have the freedom to do so. Many Christians—in particular members of the Eastern churches—have their Christmas in January. The Bible does not lock people into laws regarding such issues. Paul sets forth the principle of Christian liberty in this way: "One man considers one day more sacred than another; another man considers every day alike. Each one should be fully convinced in his own mind. He who regards one day as special, does so to the Lord. He who eats meat, eats to the Lord, for he gives thanks to God; and he who abstains, does so to the Lord and gives thanks to God" (Romans 14:5,6).

Easter and Other Holidays

Following their injunctions against the celebration of Christmas, Jehovah's Witnesses move on to other holidays. Easter is excoriated for its connection with eggs and rabbits—pagan symbols of fertility. New Year's celebrations are associated with revelry and drinking. Valentine's Day is traced back beyond St. Valentine to pagan Rome; Mother's Day is connected with ancient mother worship; and national holidays are to be avoided on the grounds that Christ's kingdom is not of this world (*Reasoning from the Scriptures* 179-80).

There is a danger in any holiday, that people get caught up in the moment and lose sight of God's blessings, his Word, and spiritual truths. But that can be said of life in general. Indeed, the Bible teaches that "the love of money is a root of all kinds of evil" (1 Timothy 6:10), yet Christians are to work, earn money, and try to use it in godly ways. Moreover, children are not to love their parents more than they love Jesus; nor are parents to place their children above him (Matthew 10:37); this does not keep Christians from having children and raising families. To cut out everything that might take one's focus from the Lord is impossible. The answer is not to steer clear of God-given and God-allowed practices. Rather, it is to live each day in close connection with God's Word.

The Bible reminds us that we enjoy the freedom to worship and celebrate when we choose. Scripture declares, "Therefore do not let anyone judge you by what you eat or drink, or with regard to a religious festival, a New Moon celebration or a Sabbath day" (Colossians 2:16).

Voting, Saluting the Flag, and Military Service

When it comes to matters that most citizens take for granted, the Witnesses again stand apart. They discourage voting and do not run for political office. They refuse to salute the flag of any country, on the grounds that such an action is tantamount to worshiping an idol. They do not sing "The Star-Spangled Banner" and other nationalistic songs. Nor are they allowed to serve in the armed forces, even when such service is compulsory (Kern 56-7).

As noted in chapter 4, during World War I, the organization's opposition to the draft led to legal action by the United States government. Judge Rutherford and his board of directors were sentenced to 20 years' imprisonment for violating the Espionage Act. They were released on bail and eventually the charges against them were dropped. In some places, most notably Nazi Germany, Witnesses have suffered greatly for their refusal to compromise their convictions regarding civil authority.

Jehovah's Witnesses consider themselves politically neutral. They argue that their allegiance belongs to God's kingdom and not to any earthly government. In keeping with this, on the front wall, behind the platform facing the congregation, each Kingdom Hall has printed the words of Acts 5:29: "We must obey God as ruler rather than men" (*New World Translation*). Members are to obey the laws under which they live, including the paying of taxes, so long as these do not violate what they consider God's law.

While Christians agree with what Acts 5:29 says, they do not accept the Witness legalistic approach to citizenship. Granted, loyalty to country is not to come before love for God. Saluting the flag, however, is neither idolizing the flag nor dishonoring God. Nor is serving in the military unchristian, in spite of what the Watchtower says.

For years, the Society allowed and even commended military service, in particular of a noncombatant nature, as an early *Watchtower* put it, there is "no command in the Scriptures against military service" (August 1, 1898, 2345). During World War II, Witnesses served in the armed forces—and returned and went to college on the GI bill (Mueller, e-mail to author). That policy has changed. Not only are Witnesses to refuse combatant service, "Jehovah's Witnesses . . . have also declined to do noncombatant service or to accept other work assignments as a substitute for military service" (*United in Worship of the Only True God* 167, quoted in Reed, *Index of Watchtower Errors* 89).

Scripture says otherwise. When soldiers came to John the Baptist for advice, he did not tell them to leave the military: "Then some soldiers asked him, 'And what should we do?' He replied, 'Don't extort money and don't accuse people falsely— be content with your pay'" (Luke 3:14). When the Roman centurion came to Jesus in Capernaum and asked him to heal his servant, Jesus declared, "I tell you the truth, I have not found anyone in Israel with such great faith" (Matthew 8:10). Christ proceeded to heal the servant of the soldier.

Jehovah's Witnesses and Mental Health

"Jehovah's Witnesses, in sticking to their unbreakable worldwide Brotherhood," declared Marley Cole back in the 1950s, "are buying a peace of mind that no one else has. It is the peace of mind that comes from believing that you are right and sticking to your convictions. It is the peace of mind of preserving integrity under stress" (244).

Studies from about that time and subsequent to it have raised serious questions about that "peace of mind." In a disturbing article, "Paradise Postponed . . . and Postponed: Why Jehovah's Witnesses Have a High Mental Illness Level," Jerry Bergman calls attention to the high incidence of "mental illness and social problems" (36). One study in America from the early 1970s found a mental illness rate among Witnesses "approximately 10 to 16 times higher than the rate for the general, non-Witness population" (38). The Christian Apologetics and Research Ministry Web site quotes a study from the *British Journal of Mental Science* that found Australian Witnesses ranking from two to four times higher among cases of schizophrenia, paranoid schizophrenia, and neurosis than the general population.

Although many Witnesses do not suffer with these troubles and no one is immune to stress and mental problems, several factors we have reviewed in our study contribute to the "nightmare" that "millions of people enter" in the Watchtower (Bergman 36).

The constant state of *doctrinal change* is one factor. Through the 1940s, for instance, vaccinations were a "direct violation" of Jehovah's law; then in the 1950s, they were "up to one's conscience"; more recently they are extolled for the lives they save (Bergman 38). We have touched on the rejection of blood transfusions, which now includes exceptions. Organ transplants are another such area. People who saw spouses die because the Society forbid transplants later saw the doctrine change to allow them (Bergman 39).

The Watchtower *theocracy* is another factor. Seeing the organization as the very voice of Jehovah and outsiders as evil produces tension. Watchtower *legalism* and *prohibitions*—announced from the theocratic hierarchy—lead to stress, including that of children being ostracized at school.

The *failure of prophecy* has done its share of damage. Couples have put off marriage or decided against having children because the end was supposedly near. The definition of "this generation" that saw 1914 and will see Armageddon keeps expanding with the passing years.

Disfellowshiping and the fear of being an outcast to friends and family creates tensions even among those who have concluded that the organization is wrong: "For this reason, many elect to stay, trudging along to Watchtower meetings and hearing and saying things that they themselves disagree with. Eventually, the inner conflict may become too great, and they have to leave, giving up family, friends, and their whole previous life" (Bergman 40).

The very acts of *witnessing* and *serving* the organization can be depressing. Bergman notes, "Doors commonly slam in their face, and although many householders are polite but not interested, some are very rude. A Witness can spend years in the field service without detecting a person who has a genuine interest in the Watchtower message!" (Bergman 41).

Barbara Grizzuti Harrison relates a story that captures much of the mental anguish of being a Jehovah's Witness. She tells of a young mother who lost two children within a year, one of whom might have been saved with a blood transfusion. The woman began to dream of seeing them in heaven, only to be criticized by fellow Witnesses who believed that outside of the 144,000, the faithful do not go to heaven, but to paradise on earth. Moreover, her grief was unbecoming a Jehovah's Witness and beginning to bother other Witnesses who "chose to see her grief as Devil-inspired apostasy" (100).

A Watchtower tract, "Comfort for the Depressed," admits that "sometimes it is impossible to defeat depression com-

144

pletely, even when everything has been tried, including medical therapies" (5). The tract holds out the promise of a paradise on earth, where there will be no more depression.

Granting that the struggle with depression can be a lifelong challenge, being a member of the Watchtower Society does more harm than good. Leaving the dark night of Watchtower legalism and entering into the sunshine of God's full, free, and complete grace is a step in the right direction. Our final two chapters will focus on this.

11. Leaving the Watchtower

> I appreciate the strengthening companionship of those I have with whom to associate . . . and hope that the future will add to my acquaintance with yet other sincere persons whose concern is for truth, not simply in doctrine, but as a way of life.
>
> I am simply trying, then, to be a Christian, a disciple of God's Son. I cannot see why anyone would want to be anything else. I cannot understand how anyone could hope to be anything more. (Raymond Franz, *Crisis of Conscience* 353)

Over the years, the Watchtower organization has had a high turnover rate, especially in the wake of failed prophecies. While it is active and aggressive in bringing new members

into the fold, there are also many leaving. Recent figures
indicate there are "about a million who have left for good"
(Wilson 11). Some of the best literature about Jehovah's
Witnesses comes from former Witnesses. Throughout our
study, we have referred to ex-Jehovah's Witnesses for the
wealth of information they offer and for their insights. We
now turn specifically to the subjects of leaving the Society
and of Christian witness to Jehovah's Witnesses.

Passages on Witnessing

Matthew 28:18-20: [Jesus said,] "All authority in heaven
and on earth has been given to me. Therefore go and make
disciples of all nations, baptizing them in the name of the
Father and of the Son and of the Holy Spirit, and teaching
them to obey everything I have commanded you. And
surely I am with you always, to the very end of the age."

Acts 1:8: [Jesus said,] "You will be my witnesses."

1 Peter 3:15: "But in your hearts set apart Christ as Lord.
Always be prepared to give an answer to everyone who
asks you to give the reason for the hope that you have.
But do this with gentleness and respect."

Former Jehovah's Witnesses Speak Out

Every religion has its share of former members who
speak out against it. What strikes this writer as unique in the
case of Jehovah's Witnesses is that there are so many of them
who take the time to write books describing their experiences. This may reflect the Watchtower penchant for the written word; more than that, it shows how serious former
Witnesses are about warning others. The bibliography at the
end of this book contains numerous works by people who
want to share their experiences and keep others from the
clutches of the organization.

In 1954, William J. Schnell left the iron clasp of the cult, and his *Thirty Years a Watchtower Slave* has become a classic in the field. Others—of varying degrees of scholarship and depth—have followed. A number of these works are included in the bibliography: Ted Dencher, *Why I Left Jehovah's Witnesses* (1966, 1980); W. C. Stevenson, *The Inside Story of Jehovah's Witnesses* (1968); Charles Trombley, *Kicked Out of the Kingdom* (1974); Barbara Grizzuti Harrison, *Visions of Glory* (1978); Joe Hewitt, *I Was Raised a Jehovah's Witness* (1979); Duane Magnani, *The Watchtower Files* (1983); Heather and Gary Botting, *The Orwellian World of Jehovah's Witnesses* (1984); M. James Penton, *Apocalypse Delayed* (1985); and Diane Wilson, *Awakening of a Jehovah's Witness* (2002). Some ex-Witnesses have devoted their careers, started help groups, and written extensively in order to enable others to see the errors of the Watchtower. David A. Reed is among those who have written numerous works on the Society.

Perhaps the most famous piece by a former member is *Crisis of Conscience* (1983) by Raymond Franz, a third-generation Witness and member of the Governing Body. Reed comments on this volume, "Although 'boring' to many non-Witness readers, *Crisis of Conscience* is so fascinating to JWs that many will read it in spite of the knowledge that they could be put on trial and punished if caught with the book in their possession. And those who do read it usually leave the organization as a result" (*How to Rescue Your Loved One* 49).

These works—and others—vary in many ways. Some emphasize the false teachings of Jehovah's Witnesses, others the mind control that the organization practices over its members. In each case, the former Jehovah's Witness points to the relief of leaving, and often the joy of finding freedom and forgiveness in Jesus Christ. With that in mind, this chapter will examine some of the testimonies of former Witnesses and outline a law-gospel approach to sharing Jesus.

149

Why They Left

In spite of their appearance of certainty, Jehovah's Witnesses might be questioning what their organization teaches. Doubts about official dogma have led some to leave the church. Ted Dencher writes, "There were three things that would not leave my mind: (1) Revelation 1:8; 22:12-16 indicated that Christ is God; (2) The *New World Translation* of John 1:1 was possibly wrong; (3) I read the Bible improperly—through Jehovah's Witnesses glasses" (84). As he searched the Scriptures, the Holy Spirit brought him to faith in his Savior.

Joe Hewitt followed a similar path: "Then I did something that was the beginning-of-the-end of my discipline as a Witness: I read the scripture in context" (32).

After years on the Society's Governing Body, Raymond Franz reached what he refers to as a "point of decision," as he saw the organization "stiffening its resistance to any Scriptural correction either as to doctrinal beliefs or its methods of dealing with those who looked to it for guidance" (224). He had come to recognize that the organization's teachings were not based on God's Word: "I could not accept that organizational interpretations, based on shifting human reasonings, could ever be made equal in authority to the actual statements found in God's unchangeable Word" (225).

After citing a number of straightforward Scripture passages, Franz refers to eight specific foundational points of the organization, not one of which is supported by Scripture. Because of the value of the information, I quote at length:

> . . . the eight points used by the Chairman's Committee as a sort of "Confession of Faith" by which to judge people had not one single point where the Society teaching involved could be supported by simple, clear-cut statements in Scripture. What plain statement in Scripture could

anyone, Governing Body member or anyone else, point to and say, "Here, the Bible clearly says":

1. That God has an "organization" on earth—one of the kind here at issue—and uses a Governing Body to direct it? Where does the Bible make such statements?

2. That the heavenly hope is not open to anyone and everyone who will embrace it, that it has been replaced by an earthly hope (since 1935) and that Christ's words in connection with the emblematic bread and wine, "Do this in remembrance of me," do not apply to all persons putting faith in his ransom sacrifice? What scriptures make such statements?

3. That the "faithful and discreet slave" is a "class" composed of only certain Christians, that it cannot apply to individuals, and that it operates through a Governing Body? Again, where does the Bible make such statements?

4. That Christians are separated into two classes, with a different relationship to God and Christ, on the basis of an earthly or a heavenly destiny? Where is this said?

5. That the 144,000 in Revelation must be taken as a literal number and that the "great crowd" does not and cannot refer to persons serving in God's heavenly courts? Where does the Bible say this?

6. That the "last days" began in 1914, and that when the apostle Peter (at Acts 2:17) spoke of the last days as applying from Pentecost on, he did not mean the same "last days" that Paul did (at 2 Timothy 3:1)? Where?

7. That the calendar year of 1914 was when Christ was first officially enthroned as King toward all the earth and that that calendar date marks the start of his parousia [Christ's second coming]? Where?

8. That when the Bible at Hebrews 11:16 says that men such as Abraham, Isaac and Jacob were "reaching out for a better place, that is, one belonging to heaven," this could not possibly mean that they would have heavenly life? Where?

Not a single Society teaching there dealt with could be supported by any plain direct statement of Scripture. Every single one would require intricate explanations, complex combinations of texts and, in some cases, what amounts to mental gymnastics, in an attempt to support them. Yet these were used to judge people's Christianity, set forth as the basis for deciding whether persons who had poured out their lives in service to God were apostates! (281-2)

Realizing the organization's lack of biblical foundation, Franz took the courageous and difficult step of resigning from his position on the Governing Body and leaving the Jehovah's Witnesses.

David Reed came to question the man-made rules of the Witnesses, especially in light of Jesus' words in Matthew 15:7-9, where he describes how the teachings of the Pharisees and teachers of the law "are but rules taught by men." He concluded that he must follow God's Word rather than the regulations of the organization: "Was I a follower of Jesus or an obedient servant to a human hierarchy?" (*Jehovah's Witnesses Answered Verse by Verse* 124). After Reed began publicly encouraging others in the organization to question the Society, he and his wife were "tried *in absentia* and disfellowshiped" (126).

152

Whither the Watchtower

As Witnesses are exposed to outside influences, they are bound to have questions. On the other hand, the Watchtower will do what it can to shelter them from the world. With a great deal of insight, Penton comments on the future of the organization:

> Although Witness leaders rightly claim that their community is growing—an important psychological factor from their standpoint—and therefore healthy, in fact it is highly unstable. The great turnover of membership, the loss of intellectuals, and, recently, the defection of many of its formerly most loyal and able members are unquestionably having an adverse affect [sic] on it. . . . Thus the community is undergoing very fundamental changes in its nature—at least in Western countries. But the organizational structure remains basically the same, and because of its fundamental conservation, the general Witness population is becoming more 'world denying,' more ghettoized, as it waits impatiently for God's day of wrath on the nations. (302)

Although the Watchtower Society has its roots in America, it is well to remember that the majority of Witnesses do not live in the United States. We should not mistake trends in the organization in the United States as affecting Witnesses everywhere.

Having said that, there do seem to be cracks in the Watchtower—especially when we consider that members have at least some awareness of the legacy of failed prophecies and changing doctrines. Even a "more 'world denying,' more ghettoized" Society is not beyond the power of the truth. Don Luke notes, "If people realized how often views did change, not many would remain in the Society" (e-mail to author). Perhaps the time is right for reaching Jehovah's Witnesses.

Sharing the Good News

Jesus tells us, "You will be my witnesses" (Acts 1:8; see also Isaiah 43:10). Fired with a desire to carry out the Great Commission and make disciples of all nations, Christians often act as if there is some magic formula to sharing our faith, as if we were selling a product and just need to find the right words. If only we say the right things and say them in the right order—so the reasoning goes—there will automatically be positive results.

It doesn't work that way. Human beings are too complex for that, and the Holy Spirit is not bound to any evangelism program, much less to a specific sales pitch. Nevertheless, there are some guidelines that can help as we share our faith with others. The following paragraphs reflect that.

Do not argue. Former Witness William Stevenson notes that "there is no point in trying to argue with the Witnesses, because they have closed minds" (198). Avoid what has been referred to as Bible ping-pong—that is, quoting Bible verses back and forth with the Witness. Ted Dencher leaves room for some verbal give and take, but adds, "You may argue with Jehovah's Witnesses, but unless you really witness for Christ you argue in vain" (84).

Do not persecute. Along with avoiding arguments, try to avoid making Witnesses feel verbally mocked or persecuted. This only reinforces their sense of mission. Hewitt comments, "'Persecuted' is a key word in the Witness vocabulary. Any time a Witness is *persecuted* it authenticates him and he is better regarded by his peers" (24). Elsewhere Hewitt says, "Don't be bitter against a brainwashed individual because of the evil his masters propagate. Instead, love him as Christ loved him, and pray for him" (191).

Give them something to think about. "Seek to plant a seed of doubt. Ask questions to make Jehovah's Witnesses think," writes Kern (13). Reed points out that rather than simply tell people, Jesus often asked questions. We can follow that same approach:

. . . if *we* provide the answers, the effect can be quite different. For example, we can tell a Jehovah's Witness: "You have been deceived!" "The Watchtower organization is a false prophet!" "You need to get saved!" but, if the Witness has not yet reached those conclusions in his own mind, he is likely to become offended and reject whatever else we have to say. So, if we want him to reach those conclusions, we must lead his thinking in that direction. Rather than comment, "Look what that verse says! It says Jesus is God!" we could ask the Witness to read the verse and then ask him, "Whom do you think the writer was referring to in this verse?" . . . What did he say about him?" and so on. The JW may not say the right answer out loud, but you will see his facial expression change when he gets the point.

Empathy is so very important when reaching out to these misled individuals. Try to think of how you would want others to speak to you, if you were the one who was misled. (*Jehovah's Witnesses Answered Verse by Verse* 115-6)

Questioning might include asking Witnesses about the false prophecies of their organization.

Encourage them to read the Bible. Having had Jehovah's Witnesses take a life of Christ course, in which there is extensive Bible reading, I have seen them come to question and think outside the box of the Watchtower. Hewitt notes:

The Watchtower Society takes scripture out of context and tries to negate the rest of the Bible, which cannot be done. . . . If you are to deal with a Witness, it is not advisable to allow him to change the subject. He is an expert at verbal gymnastics and will keep on changing the subject and traveling in circles. Make him stick with the subject at hand. Perhaps one of his doctrinal "partitions" will break down, and he will see one of the Society's contradictions, and become receptive to the gospel. (96)

Back in chapter 2, we read a passage from the *Watchtower*, which is worth considering again at this point: "From time to time, there have arisen from among the ranks of Jehovah's people those, who . . . say that it is sufficient to read the Bible exclusively. . . . But, strangely, through such 'Bible reading,' they have reverted right back to the apostate doctrines . . ." (August 15, 1981). Why do people revert back to those doctrines? It's because the Bible teaches them. Reading the Bible independently of Watchtower directives will lead people to see the truth.

Share the law and gospel. This underlies all Christian witness. The law and the gospel are the two basic doctrines of Scripture. Both can be summarized with the acronym SOS; the law *shows our sin*, and the gospel *shows our Savior*. There is a time to warn the person caught up in the way of work-righteousness that he or she can never do enough: "For whoever keeps the whole law and yet stumbles at just one point is guilty of breaking all of it" (James 2:10). This is the law. There is a time to comfort with the good news of salvation the person who is aware of his or her unworthiness: "For God so loved the world that he gave his one and only Son, that whoever believes in him shall not perish but have eternal life" (John 3:16). This is the gospel.

Speak of Christ and what he has done for our salvation. This good news, the gospel, is the most important factor in any Christian witness. Ultimately, it's all about Jesus. "Don't say, 'I am a [denomination name],'" suggests Kern. "That merely indicates to them that you are part of the devil's organization. It's better to say, 'I'm a believer in Jesus'" (11). Be kind and courteous in sharing the message of Christ. Our lives and words should reinforce each other.

The Christian and Watchtower Literature

Understanding basic beliefs of the Watchtower is important. That is just the start. When Christians do learn and try to communicate with Witnesses, more problems arise. Many Christians have become frustrated when trying to discuss biblical topics with Jehovah's Witnesses. Former Jehovah's Witness M. James Penton notes that "since their doctrines are constantly in flux, it is really impossible to discuss Witness theology in the same way that one can discuss the more stable doctrines of the great churches. Nevertheless there are certain concepts which do serve as foundations of Witness thought . . ." (159). Among those concepts are the subjects we have discussed in this book. Witnesses will appreciate it when others know something of their teachings, and that knowledge can be a factor in witnessing.

Jehovah's Witnesses will not accept Christian literature at the door, since it is considered apostate, evil, and dangerous. But what about taking their literature when they come to the door? Some suggest that Christians not accept their literature, since then instead of having to think for themselves, the Witnesses can rely on the material to answer the Christian's questions.

There are other options. One guide on witnessing suggests: "If you do accept their literature, one good strategy is to look it over, then hand it back on their next visit and say, 'I don't agree with this article. I'd really like to discuss it further with you, if you'll bring photocopies from the original sources for the quotations it uses'" (Bodine 14).

When the witness finds that the organization is not willing to furnish the requested documentation, he or she may try to find answers and thus "be taking the first steps toward breaking through his own mind-control barrier and recognizing the Watchtower Society's dishonesty for himself" (Bodine 14).

A Word of Warning

Pride comes before a fall. We've heard it and probably said it many times. We need to be careful not to forget it. The doctrinal chapters of this book (chapters 5-8) should have made it clear that while Jehovah's Witnesses have an inferior theology, they are not inferior when it comes to arguing religion. David Reed recounts how he was drawn into the Witnesses by thinking he could argue with them. All it takes is for them to convince the Christian that they are right on one point, and the "camel's nose is in the tent."

If it is important to avoid arguments with Witnesses, it is even more important not to take on several of them in small discussions. This is inviting disaster. Reed warns, "Setting out to rescue someone from a cult is serious business. It should not be approached lightly. Not only can a poorly planned attempt leave the cultist more hopelessly entrenched, but it can also put the would-be rescuer at risk" (*How to Rescue Your Loved One from the Watchtower* 153). Amy Mueller relates how after she had decided to leave the organization, she was under great pressure not to. The Society even had a former Lutheran-pastor-turned-Witness pay her a visit. Serious business indeed.

Christians need to be leery. Jehovah's Witnesses are leery. An invitation to discuss their faith and the Bible will meet with mixed results. Some will want to bring other, more knowledgeable Witnesses to the discussion. Others will simply put it off indefinitely. The subject of disfellowshiping commonly comes up among Witnesses; it is never far from the surface. They are not eager to venture out.

In the final analysis, Christians need be careful, but we need not be fearful. "For God did not give us a spirit of timidity, but a spirit of power, of love and of self-discipline" (2 Timothy 1:7). Strengthened by the Word, we can stand firm in our faith in Christ and reach out with the gospel.

12. Reaching Jehovah's Witnesses in Love

> God loves the Witnesses as He loves every sinner
> who needs Christ. Christ died for the Witnesses
> just as He did for the Hindus, Buddhists, Moslems,
> and unregenerate members of Christian churches.
> "For God so loved the world . . ." That love
> includes the victims of Watchtower brainwashing.
> (Joe Hewitt, *I Was Raised a Jehovah's Witness* 191)

Christ died for all. We have discussed how we can reflect
God's love in Christ to Witnesses, who are laboring under the
laws of their organization. We have also noted that living in a
quick-fix culture, we Christians are influenced by the mindset
that looks for simple solutions, 10- or 12- or whatever-step
programs that we can plug in and that automatically produce
results, including converting people to faith in Jesus Christ.
The same holds true when it comes to growing in the faith; it
cannot be expected to happen overnight.

The third person of the Trinity works in people's hearts
through the Word of God, through the law and gospel as they

are applied to individuals in their life situations. Individually and collectively in congregations, Christians need to do more than witness to bring people in; we also need to nurture. Jerry Bergman points out that among the people who leave the organization, "many of these become agnostics or atheists, hating God and all attempts to understand and reach Him. Some are blessed to find true spiritual and psychological recovery, however" (41). That is the goal of individual Christians and Christian congregations.

Passages on Christian Love

John 15:9,12: [Jesus said,] "As the Father has loved me, so have I loved you. Now remain in my love. My command is this: Love each other as I have loved you."

1 John 4:16,19: "God is love. Whoever lives in love lives in God, and God in him. We love because he first loved us."

1 Corinthians 13:1,13: "If I speak in the tongues of men and of angels, but have not love, I am only a resounding gong or a clanging cymbal. And now these remain: faith, hope and love. But the greatest of these is love."

Reaching Jehovah's Witnesses With Love

As we have seen, one of the harshest aspects of the Jehovah's Witness religion is the practice of disfellowshiping. Former members are shunned and disowned by their families. If churches are serious about winning and holding people who come out of this organization—and other cults and religions as well—then they must be ready to offer an alternative spiritual family to new Christians.

Severing Ties

Lifelong church members may not fully appreciate the heart-wrenching difficulties others have when leaving a cult such as that of the Jehovah's Witnesses. Raymond Franz writes of the loneliness that such a step can involve:

> Whatever the case, the Witness who follows his or her conscience may indeed find terminated virtually every friendship that he or she has had. In such circumstance, one surely needs to embrace the attitude voiced by the psalmist: "In case my own father and my own mother did leave me, even Jehovah himself would take me up." [Psalm 27:10]
>
> Only an increased awareness of God's friendship and that of his Son can compensate, can put all other relationships in proper perspective as to their relative worth. Though it may take time, there is good reason to trust that other friendships will become available, if one is willing to make the needed effort. (349)

The effort cannot be all on the part of the former Witness. He or she needs to be welcomed into a loving Christian fellowship. To break away from any cult can be not only a lonely experience but also a frightening one. Grizzutti Harrison describes the unknown aspect of stepping away from the Witnesses:

> When I left the Witnesses, I told myself that if I had to spend the rest of my life alone (believing that in all the important things, I would always be alone), the leaving would still have been worth it. I could not foresee the consequences of leaving; but I knew that the act itself was necessary, that I must try not to anticipate the consequences, and that the consequences of not acting would be worse than anything that might happen to me afterward. In all the years that followed, I never found reason to regret my decision, even through all the inescapable desolations and humiliations, the hurts and wounds that life inflicts upon us all. (385)

Clearly, leaving the Watchtower Society is a huge step. Moreover, entering a church is not an easy step either. To Jehovah's Witnesses, Christian churches are different and unfamiliar. One Witness, who happens to be married to a Lutheran, told me how strange the Lutheran services seemed to her, remarking on "all that standing up and sitting down" during a worship service.

Recognizing that outsiders are probably outside their comfort zone in a Christian church, congregations will want to offer a welcoming home to the spiritually homeless, so that none have any regrets.

Finding a Home in the Church

Sadly, too often cliquishness and coldness to outsiders and newcomers characterize Christian congregations. All the evangelism committees in the world and annual canvassing of neighborhoods and leaving doorknob hangers cannot make up for a lack of genuine love and concern. And if church membership merely means putting on a show of godliness to impress others, that is little short of unbelief. Jesus warned the Pharisees of his day—and today: "You travel over land and sea to win a single convert, and when he becomes one, you make him twice as much a son of hell as you are" (Matthew 23:15). Adding members just for the sake of increasing congregational numbers and revenue is not what it's all about.

What drives many into the cults in the first place is a desire to belong. Congregations need to reflect the love of Jesus, especially to those who are struggling with loneliness and isolation, which may be the result of becoming a Christian. Love in a Christian congregation impressed Hewitt as "more relaxed" than that in a Kingdom Hall (51). Hewitt writes about hearing Ephesians 2:8,9 in a Christian church, "I had never heard that before. But I realized that if I really were saved *it had to be by grace*. I couldn't possibly merit salvation" (62). Congregational life will reflect that grace in caring and nurturing attitudes.

In urging Christians to try to relate to Jehovah's Witnesses and value them as precious human beings, Ron Rhodes shares a touching experience:

> I remember one Sunday afternoon a Jehovah's Witness—a man about 35 years of age—stopped by my house with his son, who appeared to be about five years old. Several times during our conversation, the young boy looked up at his father admiringly. He seemed to be so proud of his father, going door to door talking to people about God. I could picture him thinking, *I'm going to be just like my dad when I grow up!*
>
> This experience, more than any other, showed me that Jehovah's Witnesses are *people* before they're *cultists.* . . . (*Reasoning From the Scriptures With the Jehovah's Witnesses* 404, italics his)

Witnesses are used to rejection, but that does not mean they ever become totally comfortable with it. Grizzuti Harrison comments, "Most of the doors were slammed in my face. So many rejections! I told myself they were rejecting Jehovah, not me. (But even now, I feel naked in front of a closed door.)" (25). Viewing other people as individuals, as blood-bought souls, will lead to open—not slammed—doors.

Former Jehovah's Witnesses and the Church

By the grace of God, Amy Mueller and Don Luke found their way out of the Watchtower and into the Lutheran church—the Wisconsin Evangelical Lutheran Synod, in particular. Throughout our study, we have shared glimpses of their stories. They speak to Christians in general—and to Jehovah's Witnesses who might be ready to listen—as they recount God's loving guidance in their lives.

Amy's Story

In telling how she left the Watchtower, Amy speaks of the need for Christians to show genuine love to Jehovah's Witnesses. She writes:

> I had always been a very good student. I had a strong desire to go to college. My parents were against the idea of a four-year institution. I had been increasingly depressed after high school. My Jehovah's Witness friends were getting married and I did not have the challenge of advanced academics anymore. When there is such a strong sense of work righteousness and legalism, it is hard not to feel guilty and resentful at the same time. After I took a one-year course at tech school my parents finally allowed me to attend a local college.
>
> While working at a local department store the summer before my freshman year, I met a Wisconsin Lutheran Seminary student through a coworker. We dated briefly without my parents' knowledge before he left for his vicar year. I think God was opening a door to the gospel because I had never defied my parents in regard to dating outside of the faith. I had never had interest in other religions, but the seminary student talked about the gospel and had such strong convictions and ideas that it surprised me. I had been raised on the arrogance that Jehovah's Witnesses were the only people who shared and lived their faith.
>
> Jehovah's Witnesses also ingrain the idea that other religions and especially their clergy are in cahoots with the devil. They are especially demonized as greedy and ignorant of Bible truths. I came to understand that although Jehovah's Witnesses are well-versed in defending their faith

through the Bible, the defenses are all dictated from the International Headquarters. They interpret the Scriptures and give direct commentary. They write the literature. They even write the sermons the elders preach. It was impressive to know that the Lutheran pastors were able to interpret Scripture directly from the original languages themselves. Among Jehovah's Witnesses, there is a unity of beliefs through complete control of information. In the Wisconsin Evangelical Lutheran Synod, there is a unity of beliefs through a true understanding of the Word of God.

After about six months of studying at the Campus Ministry I understood that I needed to leave the church. I had kept my studying a secret from my parents. I moved into my own apartment and became financially independent. About two months later, I told my parents I was joining the Lutheran church. I also sent a letter to the congregation asking to be removed as a member and informing them of my intention of joining the Lutheran church.

I knew the consequences of my actions would be enormous for me and my family. My parents refused any contact after I told them, mainly, I think, out of such deep hurt and shock. My grandparents came and begged and pleaded. I had a group of church elders come to my apartment, including a former pastor, [to] try to convince me otherwise. I think it was so painful that I repressed most of the memories. I can't really remember the time very clearly.

After almost ten years I still have limited contact with my parents. It is better than before. Last year, they met my husband. We also usually have

brief visits when we are in town. I hope with time
they will be able to overcome their hurt and be
receptive to the gospel. Being a child of God more
than compensates for the uncomfortable family
relations. (e-mail to author)

Don's Story

Rather than relate the story of his journey from the
Watchtower Society, Don Luke tells what it is like for a former
Jehovah's Witness to be a member of a Lutheran congregation.
He reminds us that arrogance is not limited to those within the
Watchtower and warns against a haughty spirit toward outsiders:

I have been to two different Lutheran churches
that had a [Bible study] series on Jehovah's
Witnesses. In each case, the people attending had
an arrogant attitude. It was like, We are right, and
they are wrong and misled. That is true, but most
Lutherans know a fraction of the Bible and in a
discussion with a Witness would be totally lost
looking up Scriptures. I have never understood
the arrogance.

What I looked for in a church was a church that
stood for right and wrong. I wanted a church that
preached God's love but also stated that we as
Christians are expected to love God and to display
that in our life.

For a variety of reasons, the Watchtower organization has
disfellowshiped many of its members. Although there may be
reinstatement after a person has been put out, that is not
always the case. Many whom the Society has expelled are
spiritually wandering, in the words of Matthew's gospel, "like
sheep without a shepherd" (9:36). Don writes about reaching
these people:

> To reach disfellowshiped Witnesses, I would talk of God's forgiveness. That will be hard for some Witnesses to grasp. Jehovah's Witnesses' "free" forgiveness is earned by works shown to the congregation and elders. After a long enough period of time a disfellowshiped person is [often] reinstated.
>
> Most of the disfellowshiped persons I have come in contact with seem to avoid any church or run wild in the world. Most have stated that they feel being a Jehovah's Witness is right but cannot live up to the standards. This would explain why so many run in the world. (e-mail to author)

The Christian church will want to offer a more caring atmosphere than does the world or other religions and cults. It is able to do this because the love of Christ is the foundation, the motivation compelling us in all we do. In the words of the apostle Paul, "Christ's love compels us" (2 Corinthians 5:14).

On Solid Rock

One of the best-known parables of Jesus is that of the wise and foolish builders (Matthew 7:24-27). The foolish man built his house on the sand, and when the rains came and the streams rose and the winds beat against that house, "it fell with a great crash." This is a picture of the person who hears Christ's words but does not put them into practice. The wise man built his house on the rock, so that when the rains came, the streams rose, and the winds blew, "it did not fall." This person hears Christ's words and puts them into practice.

Tragically, the Watchtower Bible and Tract Society is a house built on sand (see Kauffeld, *Jehovah's Witness: A House of Sand*). This is part of the frustration of dealing with Jehovah's Witnesses. As Penton writes, "Dealing with doctrinal concepts of Jehovah's Witnesses is a most difficult matter, even for one thoroughly familiar with them. The Witnesses have no systematic theology. Thus they seem unaware of many of the logical contradictions in their very complex doctrinal system and are unable to come to grips with them intellectually" (159). Add to that the changing nature of Watchtower teachings, and we truly are seeing a house built on shifting sand.

More important than arguing with the shifting assertions of Jehovah's Witnesses is being aware of the rock on which our faith rests. The psalmist asks the rhetorical question, "And who is the Rock except our God?" (18:31). Saint Paul declares, "That rock was Christ" (1 Corinthians 10:4).

The Christian Apologetics and Research Ministry observes that "critical examination of their doctrines is not encouraged by the Watchtower Organization." We ought constantly to be searching the Scriptures. In doing so, we become more firmly assured of the truths we have come to know and love.

To change metaphors for a moment, Walter Martin has compared Christians with bank tellers who are hired by the American Banking Association to detect counterfeit money. "It is most interesting that during the entire two-week training program, no teller touches counterfeit money. Only the original passes through his hands" (Martin, *Kingdom of the Cults* 16). When people are thoroughly familiar with the real thing, they can easily spot the counterfeit. Martin continues, "If the average Christian would become familiar once again with the great foundations of his faith, he would be able to detect those counterfeit elements so apparent in the cult systems, which set them apart from biblical Christianity" (16-7).

We have the real thing, the sure foundation. Throughout this book, I have consistently tried to place the real treasure alongside the counterfeit, that we might appreciate what we have in God's Word and in our Savior Jesus Christ.

On Christ, the solid rock, I stand;
All other ground is sinking sand.
(*Christian Worship* 382)

Conclusion

In researching the Jehovah's Witnesses, I could not escape the impression that the organization has passed its peak. The Society still generates a great deal of activity, devotion, and zeal. It is still large, and in other parts of the world outside its native North America, it is thriving. Yet the growth has slowed. The number of former Jehovah's Witnesses is huge. Perhaps most telling of all is that the great publishing empire continues to rely on publications from half a century ago. It's not that old writings are necessarily of less value, but there seems to be little new intellectual vigor coming from the organization.

It has to be difficult to maintain a sense of urgency when almost a century has passed since the great year of 1914, when Christ was supposed to return. And more than 30 years have gone by since 1975, the adjusted year of Christ's return. Especially since the failure of the 1975 prophecy, the organization seems to have lost some momentum.

Already back in 1984, a *Newsweek* article reported, "Many dissident members are becoming militant in their criticism of the society . . . dissidents have formed networks of former Witnesses who have been shunned by families and friends. One result is a growing body of damning literature, much of it compiled from Watch Tower files, depicting a closed, almost Orwellian society" (quoted in Magnani 9).

Much of the current Jehovah's Witness proclamation is negative—such as criticizing the celebration of Christmas and birthdays. The fact is that the organization lacks *the* great positive proclamation that would make it truly Christian, namely, Christ crucified and risen. Far from being a cause for Christians to gloat, this may be a God-given window of opportunity to reach out to souls in the Watchtower organization.

Although first written well over a quarter of a century ago, the words of the late cult researcher Walter Martin still hit home, "If evangelical Christianity continues to virtually ignore the activities of Jehovah's Witnesses, it does at the peril of countless souls. Therefore let us awaken to their perversions of Scripture and stand fast in the defense of the faith 'once delivered unto the saints' [Jude 3]" (*Kingdom of the Cults* 125).

The religion of the Watchtower is founded on the false Bible studies of its founder Charles Taze Russell. Going back into ancient history, it has revived the false teaching of the 4th-century heretic Arius. And going back to the even more distant past, it pursues the false dreams, of a heaven on earth. This was the dream of the Jews of Jesus' day, who longed for a revival of their nation's former glory. Even after Jesus rose from the dead, his disciples still asked him, "Lord, are you at this time going to restore the kingdom to Israel?" (Acts 1:6).

The Jehovah's Witness organization keeps its people motivated as they pursue the dream of a paradise on earth. Tragically, it is a false dream, for Jesus' kingdom is not of this world. "What gives Jehovah's Witnesses their dynamism, their determination to witness to God's power?" asked Marley Cole, before proceeding to answer, "Theirs is the faith and practice of universal Christianity in its pure, original form" (5). The pages of our study have shown that not to be the case, as many former Witnesses have come to realize. Our hearts go out to the thousands of Witnesses still laboring under the tyranny of the Watchtower, even as the apostle Paul's went out to his fellow Jews:

> Brothers, my heart's desire and prayer to God for the Israelites is that they may be saved. For I can testify about them that they are zealous for God, but their zeal is not based on knowledge. Since they did not know the righteousness that comes from God and sought to establish their own, they did not submit to God's righteousness. Christ is the end of the law so that there may be righteousness for everyone who believes. (Romans 10:1-4)

Jesus Christ restores the long-lost Eden, not as a paradise on earth but as an even more glorious dwelling in God's presence eternally in heaven. He has won our salvation. How eagerly we will want to share this good news—not with the thought of winning paradise but with the assurance that it has been won by Christ.

Soli Deo Gloria!

(To God Be the Glory!)

Questions for
Study and Discussion

1. Foundations of a Cult

1. What are the characteristics of a cult?

2. Why have cults proliferated over the past century?

3. Have you personally had experience with someone involved in a cult? If so, explain.

4. What distinguishes a cult from a Christian denomination?

5. What are some of the names by which the Jehovah's Witnesses' organization is known?

6. In *The Four Major Cults,* author Anthony Hoekema lists ten emphases or lessons Christians can learn from the

cults: (1) definite convictions about matters of faith; (2) importance of knowing the Scriptures; (3) zeal for witnessing; (4) use of the printed page; (5) strong sense of urgency; (6) large role assigned to laypeople; (7) sense of dedication; (8) teach definite techniques for witnessing; (9) willingness to endure ridicule; (10) relate Christian faith to good health (pages 2-8). Comment on some or all of these points.

7. How do Jesus' words in Matthew 7:15-23 apply to the cults? To "prophesy" means to proclaim God's Word not necessarily to predict the future. How are the teachings of a cult an expression of the "fruit" they bear?

2. Life in the Watchtower Society

1. Describe the control the Watchtower organization exerts over its members.

2. How does the Society view outsiders? Why is this important to keep in mind?

3. Note the various aspects of Sunday Kingdom Hall activities. How do they compare with Sunday in church?

4. What role does Watchtower literature play in the lives of Jehovah's Witnesses? Compare that with the place of books, Bible study aids, and other materials in Christian churches.

5. What are the strengths and weaknesses of the Watchtower's practice of publishing its literature anonymously?

6. Discuss the matter of openness—or lack thereof—to outside influences. How do Christians draw the line between being in the world but "not of the world"? See John 17:13-19.

7. What are the stages by which a person is drawn into the organization? Apply the saying "an ounce of prevention is worth a pound of cure." Apply the truths of Hebrews 5:11-14 and 1 Corinthians 16:13.

8. Discuss the role of discipline in the Watchtower Society. How does it compare with church discipline? Discuss the application of Matthew 18:15-20.

3. History of the Society (1): Beginnings

1. Why is understanding a religion's history important?

2. What was Charles Taze Russell's early experience with Christian churches, and how did it influence his religious development?

3. Although Russell claimed to start a Bible study organization, what unbiblical ideas were the basis for his teachings?

4. Note the religious and social atmosphere in 19th-century America. How did it affect the development of new American religious movements?

5. What similarities and differences are there between the beginning of the 20th century and the beginning of the 21st century? Observe the effect on religious or spiritual attitudes.

6. What was Russell's attitude toward mainline churches? How has that carried into the organization today?

4. History of the Society (2): From Rutherford On

1. What were some of the key events and developments in the Jehovah's Witnesses' history? Notice the role of the various leaders of the organization. What role have leaders played— and continue to play—in shaping your church body?

2. On a number of occasions, Jehovah's Witnesses have been willing to face persecution rather than compromise their beliefs, as exemplified in Nazi Germany. Some credit them with expanding or even "establishing religious freedoms in various countries" because of their insistence on holding to their political neutrality (Answers.com 3). In chapter 10, we will examine their positions more closely; for now, what might be said that is commendable about their historic attitude in regard to religious independence?

3. Already years ago, Jan Karel Van Baalen remarked, "In general it may be stated that the cults are gradually dropping some of the old belligerency: even Jehovah's Witnesses are more sparing of vehement invectives. Having obtained a hearing and a following, they no longer go about carrying a chip on their shoulder" (12). Do you agree or disagree? Comment.

4. Many Jehovah's Witnesses may not be especially aware of the history of their organization. What reason(s) might the Society have for not giving its members a deep teaching about that history?

5. What factors contributed to the rapid and worldwide growth of the Jehovah's Witnesses?

6. What challenges does the Watchtower face today?

5. The Bible and the Nature of God

1. Why was it important for Jehovah's Witnesses to develop their own translation of the Bible? Comment on some of the features of the *New World Translation.*

2. In what way(s) do Jehovah's Witnesses place reason above Scripture in their rejection of the Trinity?

3. Review the origins of the name Jehovah. Is the Society's insistence on the use of this name biblical? Why or why not?

4. Read and reflect on the account of the three visitors who came to Abraham and Sarah (Genesis 18). Who were they? Whom does Abraham recognize one of them as being?

5. Discuss the doctrine of the Trinity, citing some of the key Bible passages. Why is this doctrine so vital to Christian faith? What challenges does the doctrine present in reaching out to Jehovah's Witnesses?

6. Compare the New International Version, King James Version, or other commonly used Bible translation with that of the *New World Translation* rendering of Genesis 1:1,2: "In [the] beginning God created the heavens and the earth. Now the earth proved to be formless and waste and

there was darkness upon the surface of [the] watery deep: and God's active force was moving to and fro over the surface of the waters." What notable difference is there? How does their translation fit Watchtower theology?

7. What scriptural passages bring out the personhood of the Holy Spirit?

8. The Jehovah of the Watchtower is a deity that is neither especially mysterious nor incomprehensible. How does this god compare with the triune God of Scripture?

6. Jehovah's Witnesses and Jesus (1): Who Is Christ?

1. In what way(s) do Jehovah's Witnesses place reason above Scripture in their understanding of the Christ?

2. How has Jehovah's Witnesses' doctrine influenced the *New World Translation*?

3. Discuss some of the Old Testament messianic passages and their fulfillment in Jesus Christ. Note their portrayal of the two natures in Christ.

4. Comment on Isaiah 43:10,11, from which Jehovah's Witnesses derive their name. How does this passage relate to Jesus?

5. During his life on earth, Jesus did not make use of all of his divine powers. Give some examples.

6. Discuss some or all of the passages in this chapter and how they relate to Jesus. Comment on the strengths and weaknesses of Jehovah's Witnesses' arguments.

7. What are some of the characteristics applied equally to God and Jesus? For some examples, compare 1 Timothy 6:15 with Revelation 9:16; Psalm 23:1 with John 10:11; Isaiah 45:22,23 with Philippians 2:10,11; Psalm 18:31 with 1 Corinthians 10:4; Psalm 71:5 with 1 Timothy 1:1. For a more complete listing, see Kern, *How to Respond to Jehovah's Witnesses,* 18-21.

7. Jehovah's Witnesses and Jesus (2): Denial of Full Divinity

1. What translation and theological problems do Jehovah's Witnesses face with John 1:1?

2. Even the *New World Translation* cannot get around the simple, straightforward translation of Thomas' words to the risen Christ: "In answer Thomas said to him: 'My Lord and my God!'" (John 20:28). Witnesses have offered the explanation that Thomas looked up when he said, "My God." Or that Jesus correctly understood that he meant "a god" and so accepted this praise. What are the problems with such attempts at explanation?

3. Read the Great Commission: "Therefore go and make disciples of all nations, baptizing them in the name of the Father and of the Son and of the Holy Spirit" (Matthew 28:19). Try to read it with the Watchtower understanding of who Jesus and the Holy Spirit are. Does it still make sense? Explain your answer.

179

4. Discuss John 8:54-59 and its relation to Exodus 3:14.

5. What is the Jehovah's Witnesses' understanding of Jesus' resurrection? How does it compare with the biblical account?

6. What is the Jehovah's Witnesses' attitude toward the worship of Jesus?

7. Jehovah's Witnesses end their prayers in the name of Jesus. Does this mean that they are praying to the true God? Why or why not?

8. The End Times

1. What were some of the major false prophecies made by Jehovah's Witnesses concerning the end of the world?

2. What rationalizations do Witnesses use to explain away the Watchtower false predictions?

3. How do the many false prophecies of the Watchtower organization disqualify it as a legitimate Christian denomination?

4. Although the organization has backed off from specific date-setting, it continues to suggest that the end is just around the corner. A 1987 tract, "What Do Jehovah's Witnesses Believe?" states, "Jehovah's Witnesses are convinced that many now living will survive when God's Kingdom brings an end to all present governments and, as Noah and his family survived the Flood, they will live on

to enjoy life forever on a cleansed earth." How might such a statement draw people into the Society? Is it a scriptural statement? Explain.

5. What is the Jehovah's Witnesses' concept of Armageddon?

6. What is the difference between a Christian awareness that we are probably living in the end times and the Watchtower approach to the topic?

9. The Way of Salvation

1. What is the Watchtower view of salvation? What roles do faith and good works play? What is the Christian motivation for good works? See 2 Corinthians 5:14,15; 1 John 4:7-21.

2. Jehovah's Witnesses teach that Christ's ransom did not include Adam: "Under the Law the deliberate murderer could not be ransomed. Adam, by his willful course, brought death on mankind and hence was a murderer. (Rom. 5:12) Thus, the sacrificial life of Jesus is not acceptable to God as a ransom for the sinner Adam" (*Aid to Bible Understanding* 1373). How does such a teaching take away from the comfort of the gospel? See John 3:16 and 2 Corinthians 5:18,19. Who is included in "the world"?

3. In discussing whether or not the wicked men of Sodom will be included in the resurrection, Watchtower publications over the years have gone back and forth eight times—four saying yes, and four no (documented in Reed *Index of Watchtower Errors* 116). What does such changing of doctrine say about the Society?

181

4. Note the ways in which the Watchtower view of the afterlife differs from that of the Scriptures.

5. According to the Jehovah's Witnesses, who are the 144,000? Taking into consideration the highly symbolic nature of the book of Revelation, discuss the biblical symbolism of the 144,000 in Revelation 14:1,3.

6. In what ways is the biblical teaching about hell far stronger than the Witness teaching of annihilation?

7. In what ways is the biblical teaching of heaven more comforting than that of the Witnesses?

10. Christian Freedom Versus Legalism

1. Define the concept of religious legalism and contrast it with the concept of Christian liberty.

2. Take note of the "torture stake" versus "cross" controversy. Why is it significant?

3. Is the Jehovah's Witness rejection of holiday and birthday celebrations biblical? Explain your answer.

4. In what ways might Christians distinguish the true celebration of Christmas and Easter from the worldly perversions of these holidays?

5. What is the scriptural position on military service and loyalty to one's country? See Romans 13:1-7.

6. How has the Watchtower Society created tragic situations with its positions on medical issues?

7. Note some of the changes in Watchtower doctrine over the years. What accounts for such fluctuations? Why are they troubling to people?

11. Leaving the Watchtower

1. Although the Jehovah's Witnesses are active and growing, what does their high turnover rate say about the organization?

2. What are some of the reasons so many people have left the Watchtower organization? How might an understanding of them help in witnessing to Jehovah's Witnesses?

3. What are some of the positive biblical truths that Christians should emphasize when sharing their faith with Jehovah's Witnesses?

4. In what respects do people have to be ready to leave the organization before any outsider can reach them?

5. Can anyone be argued out of (or into) a religion? Explain your answer.

6. Who alone can bring people to faith? See 1 Corinthians 12:3. By what means does this come about? See Romans 10:17.

7. Make note of and discuss some of the guidelines on what to do or not to do in witnessing. In *Reasoning From the Scriptures With Jehovah's Witnesses,* author Ron Rhodes lists four do's and two don'ts:

> Do identify with the Jehovah's Witness.
>
> Do labor persistently with the Jehovah's Witness.
>
> Do exhaust every effort to answer the questions of Jehovah's Witnesses.
>
> Do allow the Jehovah's Witness to save face.
>
> Don't approach a Jehovah's Witness with a spiritual [condescending] chip on your shoulder.
>
> Don't lose your patience, regardless of how dense you may think the Jehovah's Witness is. (403-8)

Comment on the value of these suggestions. Share personal experiences you may have had.

12. Reaching Jehovah's Witnesses in Love

1. In our lives and in our witnessing, note the value of our personal example. See 1 Peter 3:15,16.

2. Have you had any exchanges with Jehovah's Witnesses? If so, what were they? What did you learn from them?

3. In *Thirty Years a Watchtower Slave,* William Schnell advises that when you have politely heard a Witness out, without arguing or even answering, "Tell him what the

Lord Jesus means to you: give him your testimony. Make it short and sweet, but say it with enthusiasm. Then ask the JW to give you his testimony. This will nonplus him— he cannot speak of the grace of God in Jesus Christ" (191). Discuss the value of a positive witness for Christ.

4. Why is it not enough for Witnesses simply to leave the Watchtower organization?

5. Why is Christian love so important in reaching out to people and in keeping them in a Christian congregation?

6. What practical programs might churches apply to make all members feel that they belong? What might be done for inquirers and new members?

7. What can you personally do to reach Jehovah's Witnesses— and others—with the saving gospel of Jesus Christ?

185

Appendix

The Arian Controversy

"There is nothing new under the sun," wrote wise King Solomon almost three thousand years ago (Ecclesiastes 1:9). While relatively new among large religious bodies, the Jehovah's Witness organization has its roots in an ancient heresy regarding the nature of Jesus Christ. Known as the Arian Controversy, this theological debate led to the first and greatest church council and helped crystallize for all time the church's understanding of the biblical teachings concerning the two natures in Christ.

The Early Church

The story goes back to the 4th century and has its origins even further back than that. During its first centuries, the Christian faith spread rapidly from its center in Jerusalem throughout the Mediterranean world of the Roman Empire. During many of those early years of rapid expansion, Christianity was a persecuted faith, for it stood in opposition to the pantheon—the gods and goddesses—that made up the official state religion of the Romans.

Finally, in the early 4th century, the Roman Emperor Constantine I legitimized the Christian religion and gave it favored status. Literally overnight, the church went from being persecuted to being legal and even privileged. Constantine, who established his capital in the city he named after himself (Constantinople—modern Istanbul), became a Christian and was baptized on his deathbed.

It was also during the first three centuries that the inspired writings of the New Testament were gradually coming together into the compilation of 27 books we know as the canon. The books were known and recognized throughout the church, but having been written for widely scattered audiences, they had not yet been gathered into one collection.

Those books, in keeping with the Old Testament prophetic books that spoke of the coming Messiah, describe the Savior Jesus Christ as true God and true man. This is the doctrine of the incarnation, as John's gospel puts it, "The Word became flesh and made his dwelling among us" (1:14). Yet what does it mean that Jesus is the God-man? How can the indescribable be described?

Around the discussion of such questions swirled the so-called christological controversies of the early church. The greatest, most far-reaching, and most famous was the Arian Controversy.

The Arian Controversy

The term *Arian* refers to the followers of a Christian priest named Arius, who lived in Alexandria Egypt in the early 4th century. He believed and taught that Jesus was not coeternal with God the Father but that Jesus was a created being and thus inferior to the Father. "Even if He [Jesus] is called God," wrote Arius, "He is not God truly" (Hoekema, 327).

Such beliefs called into question the very doctrines of the Trinity and the divinity of Christ. In the year 321 in Alexandria, a synod (a gathering of church leaders) condemned the views of Arius as heterodox, that is, heretical. Nevertheless, Arius and his supporters were highly influential in the schools of Alexandria and soon gained a wide following throughout the eastern Mediterranean world, causing turmoil throughout the churches and involving everyone from the church hierarchy to the man on the street.

Disturbed by the growing factionalism throughout the empire, Emperor Constantine called for a council of church leaders in 325 to deal with the situation. This was the Council of Nicaea, the first of the church-wide or ecumenical councils. Centuries later, Luther would refer to this as "the most sacred of all councils" (White, "What Really Happened at the Council of Nicea?" 30).

A mere 14 years after the church had suffered its last persecution, about 318 bishops, mostly from the Eastern part of the empire, gathered at Nicaea, near Constantinople. Bedecked in gold and gems, Constantine himself entered the assembly and presided over it. Church historian Philip Schaff notes the irony:

> How great the contrast between this position of the church and the time of the persecution but scarcely passed! What a revolution of opinion in bishops who had once feared the Roman emperor as the worst enemy of the church, and who now greeted the same emperor in his half barbarous attire as an angel of God from heaven, and gave him, though not yet even baptized, the honorary presidency of the highest assembly of the church! (625)

Some historians contend that the council was political, that Constantine pushed through his agenda, and that the very notion of the Trinity came into being at this time. In recent times, these ideas have been widely circulated, in particular by a best-selling novel and the movie based on it, *The Da Vinci Code*. While Constantine was interested in harmony

189

within his empire, it was the bishops who ultimately had to deal with the sacred truths at hand.

The Watchtower book *"Babylon the Great Has Fallen!" God's Kingdom Rules* asks, "But why should these overseers, if they were Christians, obey a pagan Pontifex Maximus [Constantine] and let him dictate in Christian matters?" (477). The answer supplied is that they were intimidated by the emperor's entourage. In fact, as even the Witness publication points out, in his later years Constantine leaned toward the Arians, being baptized by an Arian supporter. Scripture determined the outcome.

There were three views presented at Nicaea:

1. Jesus is of the *same substance* as the Father (Greek *homoousios*), the orthodox view held by Athanasius.

2. Jesus is of a *similar substance* to the Father (Greek *homoiousios*), the majority position, held by middle-of-the-road theologians, and advocated by the church historian Euebius.

3. Jesus is of *different substance* from the Father (Greek *heteroousios*), the view of Arius and his party.

Only one little letter (the Greek *iota*; the "smallest letter" of Matthew 5:18) separated the first two views. It came down to the question of whether Jesus is substantially *like* God or in substance is God. The Arians held that Jesus is a created creature.

Although at first a minority, the orthodox party had the most gifted spokesmen, in particular the young Athanasius. They helped the middle party to a deeper understanding of the issues (Schaff 627-8). When a statement of faith was drawn up, only Arius and two bishops declined to sign it. The decision was not political but scriptural. For Constantine had been more interested in peace than in a particular outcome. In "What Really Happened at the Council of Nicea?" James White summarizes the outcome, "There was one reason the Nicene definition prevailed: its fidelity to the testimony of the Scriptures" (32).

Contrary to common ideas about this controversy, it did not end with the declaration at Nicaea. The Arians remained strong and for a time even prevailed. Arius was acquitted of heresy; he died at the age of 80-some years (in 336), on the night before he was to take part in a royal procession in Constantinople in recognition of his reception back into the church. On the other hand, the brilliant Athanasius, who became bishop of Alexandria shortly after the council, was removed from his position five times.

After years of turmoil, when it often seemed that the orthodox cause was lost, another council was held. Almost 60 years after Nicaea, the Council of Constantinople (381) reaffirmed the orthodox, scriptural position. For several centuries, however, Arianism did continue in Western Europe among some Germanic tribes, such as the Goths, having been brought there by the Arian missionary Ulfilas.

Delving deeply into the Scriptures—in contrast to Arius, who drew upon human reason—Athanasius recognized what was at stake. In the person of Jesus Christ, the almighty God has bridged the gap between himself and sinful man. This was not done through some intermediary but by God himself entering into our world. Such is the wonder and the grandeur of the incarnation.

The Nicene Creed

The word *creed* is from the Latin word *credo,* which means "I believe." A creed is a statement of faith. The three ecumenical (or worldwide) creeds reflect the scriptural teachings regarding the Trinity and the person of Jesus Christ. Those creeds are the Apostles' Creed, the Nicene Creed, and the Athanasian Creed.

Although named after the apostles and the great church father Athanasius, the creeds that bear their names were not written by them. Nevertheless, they do reflect their teachings. From the first ecumenical council, that of Nicaea (A.D. 325), and the later Council of Constantinople (A.D. 381) arose the Nicene Creed, which emphasizes the deity of Christ in opposition to Arianism and other christological errors. It is well to review this creed for the timeless truths it expresses:

> We believe in one God, the Father, the Almighty,
>> maker of heaven and earth,
>> of all that is,
>> seen and unseen.
> We believe in one Lord, Jesus Christ, the only Son of God,
>> eternally begotten of the Father,
>> God from God, Light from Light, true God from true God,
>> begotten, not made,
>> of one being with the Father.
> Through him all things were made.
> For us and for our salvation, he came down from heaven,
>> was incarnate of the Holy Spirit and the virgin Mary,
>> and became fully human.
> For our sake he was crucified under Pontius Pilate.
> He suffered death and was buried.
> On the third day he rose again in accordance with the
>> Scriptures.
> He ascended into heaven
>> and is seated at the right hand of the Father.
> He will come again in glory to judge the living and the dead,
>> and his kingdom will have no end.
> We believe in the Holy Spirit,
>> the Lord, the giver of life,
>> who proceeds from the Father and the Son,

who in unity with the Father and the Son is worshiped
and glorified,
who has spoken through the prophets.
We believe in one holy Christian and apostolic Church.
We acknowledge one baptism for the forgiveness of sins.
We look for the resurrection of the dead
and the life of the world to come. Amen.
(*Christian Worship 18-9*)

Jehovah's Witnesses and Arius

Charles Taze Russell honored Arius as one of the great teachers of Christian history. According to the April 1, 1919, *Watchtower,* there were seven messengers of the church: Saint Paul, Saint John, Arius, Waldo, Wycliffe, Luther, and Russell (Penton 181). All except the first two stood in opposition to the organized church. As for Luther, although the Reformation brought about some positive changes such as the translation of the Bible into the language of common people, the Protestant churches kept the Trinity, the immortal soul, and hell (*Jehovah's Witnesses: Proclaimers of God's Kingdom* 39-40).

Today, Arianism lives on in the teachings of the Watchtower Bible and Tract Society. This is not to say that their teachings are identical. Unlike the Witnesses, Arius did not contend that Jesus was the archangel Michael; and he believed in the personhood of the Holy Spirit (Hoekema 328). Nevertheless, in their denial of the divinity of Jesus, the Witnesses are present-day Arians.

Vocabulary

Adams, Don. Elected sixth Watchtower Bible and Tract Society (WBTS) president in 2000, at the age of 75.

Annihilation. The doctrine that unbelievers will not be eternally punished; they will instead be annihilated. This will occur after the probation of the millennium.

Anointed Class. The 144,000 Jehovah's Witnesses chosen by God to rule in heaven with Jesus after they die on earth. Witnesses contend that only this limited number of people will live in a spiritual heaven with King Jesus. All other faithful Jehovah's Witnesses will live on a paradiselike earth. Also known as Bride of Christ, Faithful and Discreet Slave, Little Flock.

Apostate. One who leaves the Watchtower Society and joins another church, thus rejecting Jehovah's Witness beliefs. Considered worse than simply disassociating oneself. *See also* Evil Slave.

Arius. Early Christian heretic who affirmed that there was a time when the Son of God was not. Though he was repudiated by the Council of Nicaea in 325, he was regarded by Charles Taze Russell as one of the six great Christian teachers before himself.

Armageddon. War to rid the earth of wickedness and to save faithful Witnesses; impending battle between the hosts of Christ and Antichrist, which will issue in the destruction of the latter. Centered in Palestine (Israel), a total world battle will take place, and all people and institutions not affiliated with Jehovah's Witnesses will be destroyed, with the churches of Christendom being the first to go. Jesus and his heavenly host will defeat Satan and his armies.

Assembly. Many congregations coming together for an all-day meeting, usually held twice each year under the direction of the Watchtower Society.

Awake! One of the major publications of the Watchtower Bible and Tract Society. A semimonthly family magazine, which features articles of human interest, religion, and practical topics.

Back calls. A Jehovah's Witness visitor will make return calls if a person shows even a little interest or requests more information on the initial visit. WBTS encourages persistent visitation.

Baptism. Water immersion of an individual by a brother in good standing, symbolizing dedication to Jehovah through a commitment to the Watchtower Society; a requirement to become a Jehovah's Witness and to survive Armageddon. A candidate approved by WBTS is immersed in water during a public meeting—usually a circuit assembly; mass baptisms are also conducted and candidates may number in the hundreds. Infant baptism is considered false doctrine. Children are baptized when they are thought to have reached the age of accountability; before that they are saved by their parents' faith.

Beth-Sarim. The "House of Princes," in San Diego, California, until 1948, maintained by the Witnesses as a residence for Old Testament saints who had been expected to return. They are still expected to return, but they will apparently have to find their own accommodations now because of their belated arrival.

Bethel. Official world headquarters of the Watchtower Society in New York, and main printing factory for the organization's literature; located at 25 Columbia Heights, Brooklyn, New York.

Bible Students. Original name of Jehovah's Witnesses.

Bible study. Regular one-on-one meetings in the home of a person who wants to learn the teachings of Jehovah's Witnesses; study of the Watchtower Society's interpretation of the Bible, using Watchtower literature and taught by a Witness. Jehovah's Witnesses profess a literal belief in the Bible and seek to engage interested people in home Bible studies.

Birthdays. Celebrating a birthday in any way is strictly forbidden. Even sending a birthday card can bring action against the offender by an official judicial committee. The punishment is disfellowshiping.

Blood. The soul is in the blood (Leviticus 17:11,14). Blood is sacred because life is sacred. The only proper use of blood is sacrifice (Leviticus chapter 11).

Blood transfusions. Accepting a blood transfusion—"eating blood"—is considered a sin more serious than theft or adultery. A Witness must refuse blood, even when this is certain to result in death. The organization also requires adults to refuse transfusions for their minor children.

Bloodguilt. Guilt is acquired by bloodshed, including support of a blood-guilty organization such as Babylon the Great (see Revelation 14:8); eating or drinking blood in any way (Acts 15:20); or failing to preach the good news of the kingdom (Acts 18:6).

Bloodguilty. State of being responsible for the loss of one or more human lives.

Book study. Weekly gathering of Witnesses to discuss Watchtower Society publications.

Branch committee. Committee appointed by WBTS with general oversight of the Jehovah's Witnesses congregations in an entire country or group of countries.

Bride of Christ. *See* Anointed Class.

Brother. Male baptized Jehovah's Witness.

Brothers. Male baptized Jehovah's Witnesses collectively; also a term that is sometimes used when referring to the elder body or the leaders in the organization.

Christ. *See* Jesus Christ.

Christ's return. The Lord returned invisibly in 1914 and has been present ever since, ruling as King on earth through the Watchtower Society. References to the second "coming" are rendered as "presence" in the Jehovah's Witness Bible. The generation of people who witnessed Christ's invisible return in 1914 will not pass away before Armageddon comes (see Matthew 24:34).

Christendom. All religions that profess to be Christian (excluding Jehovah's Witnesses); the Society views these as false Christianity. This derogatory term refers to Protestant and Catholic groups, which are thought to have been established in the 4th century by the unbaptized Roman emperor Constantine the Great. According to Jehovah's Witnesses, except for a few scattered individuals who kept the faith, true Christianity vanished from the earth shortly after the death of the apostles. It was not restored until Charles Taze Russell set up the Watchtower organization. When Christ returned invisibly in 1914, he found Russell's group doing the work of the "faithful and discreet slave" (Matthew 24:45) and appointed them over all his belongings. Other churches and professed Christians are tools of the devil.

Christian. Jehovah's Witnesses exclusively.

Chronology. A timetable for past and future events, tied together by mathematical formulas and revealed to mankind through the Watchtower Society. The seven "days" of the Genesis creation account were each 7,000 years long, for a total "week" of 49,000 years. God created Adam in the year 4026 B.C. His creation of Eve a short time later marked the end of the sixth creative day and the beginning of the seventh. We are now approximately six thousand years into that seven thousand–year period—which means that Armageddon will soon put an end to six thousand years of human struggle, making way for a Sabbath-like thousand-year reign of Christ. On the basis of this chronology, the Society has set forth a number of specific end-times prophecies.

Circuit. Group of about 20 congregations.

Circuit assembly. Member congregations of the circuit gather at specified times for fellowship, inspiration, and indoctrination. The sessions are usually held in a public facility. Mass baptisms of new converts are often conducted at these meetings.

Circuit overseer. A traveling elder appointed by the Society to supervise a circuit. This official leader of the circuit visits each congregation two or three times a year, usually staying a week at a time.

Committee. *See* Judicial Committee.

Company. Another name for a Jehovah's Witness congregation.

Congregation. A group of Witnesses who regularly meet together under the leadership of one or more elders and the direction of the Watchtower Society. Group of no more than two hundred Witnesses meeting at a Kingdom Hall.

Consolation. A popular periodical of the Russellites.

Convention. Large Jehovah's Witness gathering of several circuits lasting from three to seven days held yearly under the direction of the Society.

Cross. A pagan religious symbol adopted by the church when Satan took control of ecclesiastical authority. It had nothing to do with Christ's death; Jehovah's Witnesses maintain that he was nailed to a straight upright pole, a "torture stake," without a crossbeam. Witnesses abhor the cross, and new converts are expected to destroy any crosses they may have. *See also* Impalement.

Cult. A non-Christian religion, denying the Trinity and divinity of Jesus; often having a dynamic leader, strongly controlled members, and emphasis on work-righteousness as the way of salvation.

Day of Our Lord Jesus Christ. Jehovah's Witnesses say this time period began when Christ returned to his temple, probably in 1918. It continues until Armageddon.

Death. Termination of existence.

Dedication. Commitment to the Watchtower organization preceding Baptism.

Deity. The Father alone is God, and true worshipers must call him by the name Jehovah. Witnesses believe that Jesus Christ was merely a manifestation of Michael the archangel in human form—not God but a created being. The Holy Spirit is thought of as neither God nor a person but as an "active force." *See also* Jehovah.

Demons. Angels who chose to follow Satan; the devil and the demons were ousted from heaven down to the earth in 1914.

Devil. *See* Lucifer, Satan.

Disassociation. Voluntary removal of oneself from the Watchtower Society. Viewed by Witnesses as suicide, since they believe Jehovah will forever destroy disassociated persons at Armageddon. Viewed also as turning one's back on Jehovah and choosing the devil's side; Witnesses are required to shun disassociated persons. *See also* Disfellowshiping, Expelling.

Disfellowshiping. Involuntary, forced removal by the elders of a person from the organization (excommunication) for biblical wrongdoing or violation of the organization's rules. It consists of a public decree, announced at a Kingdom Hall meeting and prohibiting all association or fellowship with the offender. Viewed by Witnesses as a death sentence if the person does not repent and return to the organization. Witnesses are to shun a disfellowshiped person and are forbidden even to say hello if they encounter the offender on the street. The only exceptions are that family members may conduct necessary business with a disfellowshiped person, and elders may speak to him if he approaches them repentantly to seek reinstatement. Suspension is usually for one year; then the offending member is given the opportunity for reinstatement. *See also* Disassociation, Expelling.

District. Organization of about ten circuits.

District overseer. Leader supervising several circuits and responsible for conducting circuit assemblies. He spends one week in the circuit for each assembly held.

Divine life. Life of the highest order, like that of Jehovah God. Reserved for Jesus and the Anointed Class.

Elder. A "scripturally qualified" brother appointed by the Society as leader in a congregation, at times likened to a pastor in a church. An elder follows the recommendations of the local body of elders. Friendship and family networks are often important in this process. There is no limit to the number of elders a congregation may have.

Elder Body. All of the elders in a congregation.

Emblems. The unleavened bread and wine, symbolizing Jesus' body and blood, which are circulated among the congregation members during the annual celebration of the Memorial.

End (The). Armageddon, bringing an end to the world as we know it.

Everlasting death. Annihilation.

Everlasting life. Life in a perfect organism, fleshly for humans who gain life on earth, spiritual for faithful angels who continue to live in heaven.

Evil slave. Former Witness who openly opposes the Watchtower Society.

Expelling. Also referred to as excommunication or disfellowshiping. Members may be expelled for several reasons, including adultery, homosexuality, greed, dishonesty, drunkenness, murder, idolatry, apostasy, and divisiveness. An offending member may be received back if he or she displays sincere repentance. *See also* Disassociation, Disfellowshiping.

Faith. The sum of beliefs concerning Jehovah God and his Kingdom. Maintaining faith requires putting up a fight; resisting those who could lead one into immorality; combating the works of the flesh; avoiding materialism, faith-destroying philosophies, and traditions of men; and looking attentively to Jesus.

Faithful and Discreet Slave (or Servant). The Society's interpretation of Matthew 24:45, where Jesus predicted that God would establish a special "slave" or "servant" on earth, having the spiritual authority to represent him and acting as the sole interpreter of the Bible. The Watchtower organization, as represented by the Governing Body, applies this designation to itself. *See also* Anointed Class.

Fasting. Abstaining from food and drink; neither commanded nor prohibited.

Field service. Jehovah's Witnesses' house-to-house preaching, distribution of Watchtower literature, and conducting of home Bible studies with interested persons who are not Witnesses.

Franz, Frederick W. Elected fourth WBTS president in 1977; he died in 1992 at the age of 99. Key figure in developing the *New World Translation* of the Bible.

Gehenna. New Testament Greek word, derived from the Hebrew, indicating place of endless punishment; but according to Jehovah's Witnesses, annihilation. The term is associated with the dump outside ancient Jerusalem where trash was burned; Witnesses say Christendom has turned this into the false doctrine of hell. *See also* Hades, Hell.

Gentile times. Jehovah's Witnesses believe this is the period from 607 B.C. to A.D. 1914 when Jews were in disfavor with Jehovah.

Gifts of the Spirit. Paul lists nine manifestations of the Spirit. They are not to be used for selfish profit. Speaking in tongues is considered a lesser gift and is only used when someone can interpret.

Gilead. Missionary school of the Watchtower Society.

Goat. Someone opposed to the message of Jehovah's Witnesses.

Goodwill person. A person who is interested in Bible study and is a prospective member of Jehovah's Witnesses. Those who are not interested are called goats. *See also*, more commonly used, Interested.

Governing Body. Central group of experienced elders who oversee the worldwide congregation. A group varying from 11 to 17 anointed Witness men residing at the Watchtower headquarters in New York, claiming to be enlightened by Jehovah, the sole interpreter of the Bible, and the only channel of communication between God and humankind. The Governing Body determines what all Jehovah's Witnesses are required to believe and obey.

Great Crowd. The multitude of people who are faithful to Jehovah but not selected for heavenly life. They will survive Armageddon and live in the "new system" or paradise established on earth.

Great Tribulation. Time of great trouble and anguish on the earth directly preceding Armageddon, marked by the attack of the world's governments—led by the United Nations—on Jehovah's Witnesses.

Hades. Word sometimes used in the Bible to refer to death as the separation from the world; Jehovah's Witnesses see in it a denial of hell. Watchtower literature says this Greek word refers to the common grave of all mankind, where the dead and buried are unseen. It corresponds to the Hebrew term *Sheol*. *See also* Gehenna, Hell.

Har Magedon. Variant spelling of *Armageddon* used in Watchtower literature. *See also* Armageddon.

Harp of God. Judge Rutherford's basic and comprehensive elucidation of Jehovah's Witness theology.

Heaven. Only 144,000 will go to heaven. This "little flock" began with the 12 apostles, and the number was filled by the year 1935, with the rest of the Jehovah's Witnesses hoping to live in paradise on earth.

Hell. Common grave of mankind. Hades is merely the grave; the fire of Gehenna instantly disintegrates its victims into nothingness; and there is no conscious existence for the dead until the time of their bodily resurrection. Witnesses do not believe it is a place of torment or fire. They reject the doctrine of eternal punishment, saying all non-Jehovah's Witnesses will be annihilated at the final judgment. *See also* Gehenna, Hades.

Henschel, Milton G. Elected fifth WBTS president in 1992, at the age of 73; he resigned in 2000 and died in 2003.

Holidays. Celebration of many holidays is forbidden for Jehovah's Witnesses. This prohibition applies to US presidents' birthdays, Valentine's Day, Memorial Day, Christmas, Easter, New Year's Day, Thanksgiving, Good Friday, Mother's Day, and Father's Day. Even if a pagan origin cannot be found for a particular observance, many such celebrations are forbidden because they glorify the individual rather than God. Anniversaries are usually commemorated, with large parties often held for silver and golden anniversaries.

Holy Spirit. A divine force, not a person as in trinitarian Christianity. The Holy Spirit is neither God nor a person, according to Watchtower teaching. It is simply an impersonal active force that God uses in doing his will.

Hope. Formerly it was taught that God stopped calling Christians to a heavenly hope in the year 1935. Since then, God has been offering people the opportunity to live forever on this earth. "Millions now living will never die" is a common Witness slogan. God will destroy everyone else, leaving only Jehovah's Witnesses, and he will restore an Edenic paradise for them. The current Watchtower position is that while most of the 144,000 have already been called to heaven, it is possible for some younger people to be among that number. This helps explain the transition of younger men into the Governing Body.

Immortality. Jehovah's Witnesses teach an earthly and heavenly immortality.

Impalement (of Jesus). WBTS says the Greek term *stauros* in both Koine and classical Greek carries no thought of a cross made of two timbers. Witnesses believe it simply means an upright stake, with the idea of a two-piece cross being adopted from pagans in the 3rd century. *See also* Cross.

Incarnation. A clothing, or state of being clothed, with flesh; taking on, or being manifested in, a body of flesh; the condition of angels appearing to mankind on earth. Witnesses believe that the Nephalim people of Noah's day (Genesis 6:4) were very large because they were the offspring of fallen angels and earthly women. Not the incarnation of Christianity, in which God the Son takes on flesh and blood.

Interested. A person who is interested in Bible study and is a prospective member of Jehovah's Witnesses. Those who are not interested are called goats. *See* Goodwill person.

International Bible Society. This group supervises Jehovah's Witness ministries in Canada and England.

Jehovah (also Jehovah God). According to Jehovah's Witnesses, the name of the only true God, strongly emphasized by Witnesses; the Father of Jesus Christ. Greatest Personality in the universe, Creator; not triune; not omnipresent. *See also* Deity.

Jehovah's Witnesses. Baptized members of the Watchtower Society, believing themselves to be God's chosen servants and the only true Christians on earth.

Jesus Christ. A created being; Michael the Archangel—the first one that God created when he started creating angels. Witnesses also call Jesus "the Son of God" and "a god" and translate John 1:1 accordingly in their Bible. *See also* Michael.

Jonadabs. Members of the Jehovah's Witnesses who come into the organization to escape the approaching storm of Armageddon. They are not considered Christians, but they are taught that if they stay within the confines of the organization, follow all its instructions, listen attentively to Watchtower indoctrination, regularly go out as publishers, and report the time they spend in doing so, then perhaps they will be saved in Armageddon. This is an older term, and young Jehovah's Witnesses may not be familiar with it.

Judicial Committee. Meeting of three elders appointed to conduct a hearing (or trial) with a Witness who is accused of breaking the organization's rules, or of committing a biblical wrongdoing.

Kingdom Hall. Meeting place and house of worship of Jehovah's Witnesses; usually simple and austere. Many of these buildings were built entirely by volunteer labor and with the exception of the foundation, completed in the course of a weekend.

Kingdom of God. The capital or ruling part of God's universal organization; comprised of King Christ Jesus and 144,000 associate kings taken from among men. It is entirely heavenly, having no earthly part. All members must be resurrected and given spirit bodies. The Kingdom began operation in full power with the enthronement of Christ in the heavens 1917. All selected for the Kingdom must die in order to enter it.

Kingdom publishers. Majority of Jehovah's Witnesses. Expected to spend five hours per week at meetings in the Kingdom Hall and as much time as possible witnessing. *See also* Publisher.

Kingdom-ruling associates. No others besides the Kingdom members in heaven receive incorruptibility and immortality.

Knorr, Nathan H. Born in 1905 and elected third WBTS president in 1942, he died in 1977.

Last days. The time between Christ's return in 1914 and Armageddon.

Little Flock. Another name for the 144,000 Witnesses who inherit eternal life in heaven. *See also* Anointed Class.

Lucifer. The second-born creature of God (after the firstborn, Jesus), who rebelled and has become the chief adversary of Jehovah; he will be destroyed in the Battle of Armageddon. *See also* Satan.

Man of Lawlessness. The collective clergy of Christendom.

Marked. Label applied to Witnesses who are guilty of disobeying the Society's rules but not seriously enough to warrant disfellowshiping. Witnesses who are marked are socially ostracized.

Marked generation. People living in the time period from 1914 onward. This time period is marked in that some of the people born in 1914 will live to experience Armageddon.

Memorial. Mandatory yearly observance of the Lord's Evening Meal, sometimes compared to Communion in many churches. Only Witnesses of the Anointed Class of 144,000 may partake of the bread and wine, while others in attendance simply observe, although everyone takes part in passing the bread and wine around.

Messenger of the Covenant. Another name for Christ.

Michael. The archangel, firstborn creature, who is the leader of Jehovah's hosts and at one time became the man, Jesus. *See also* Jesus Christ.

Millennium. According to Jehovah's Witnesses, a period of one thousand years that follows Armageddon and consists of paradise on earth for the faithful survivors and a selected group of resurrected people. The coming visible reign of Christ on earth during which an effective enforced peace will prevail and evangelization will be accelerated.

Minister. Baptized Jehovah's Witness publisher.

Ministerial servant. A brother appointed by the elder body to assist the elders. The scriptural requirements for ministerial servant are fewer than those for elders.

New light. New information or insights regarding Watchtower doctrine that Witnesses believe to be channeled from God to the Society's Governing Body and presented through the Society's literature or speakers at Watchtower conventions or assemblies.

New Order. *See* New System.

New System. The paradise that God will restore to earth after Armageddon, where obedient humankind will live forever under God's rule as administered on earth through the Watchtower Society. Often referred to as the New Order.

New World Translation of the Holy Scriptures **(NWT).** Official translation of the Old and New Testaments by WBTS. In some cases, conventional translations of passages are changed to fit Jehovah's Witness theology.

NWT. *New World Translation of the Holy Scriptures,* the Watchtower Society's own translation of the Bible.

Old World. The current world ruled by Satan prior to Armageddon.

Organization (The). The Watchtower Society, including all the congregations of Jehovah's Witnesses, its leaders, headquarters, branch offices, and printing facilities. It lays claim to being God's sole organization and the only true religion on earth. Witnesses believe that God set up the Watchtower organization as his channel of communication to gather those who will be saved. As God's visible agency on earth, this organization exercises full governmental authority over believers—it promulgates laws, puts violators on trial, operates Kingdom schools, and so on—parallel to the secular government. If there is a conflict between the two, the organization is to be obeyed, rather than secular rulers. *See also* Society.

Other Sheep. *See* Great Crowd.

Overseer. Term formerly referring to an exemplary brother chosen by the Society to lead, supervise, and shepherd a congregation, similar to a pastor in a church; this arrangement was later replaced by a body of elders. Term still used to describe the position of leadership over assemblies, conventions, circuits districts, and branches.

Paradise. Eden, achieved by work of Jehovah's Witnesses on earth after Armageddon.

People's Pulpit Association. The first Jehovah's Witness president organized this movement in 1909. The name was changed to the Watchtower Bible and Tract Society in 1939.

Pioneer publisher. An exemplary, voluntary, full-time Jehovah's Witness minister whose field service is regularly 100 hours a month (later lowered to 90 hours a month), also holding part-time jobs while serving as lay clergy.

Placements. Watchtower Society literature given to a non-Witness or left at homes or public places for people to read.

Platform. The stage in the Kingdom Hall from which brothers deliver lectures or address the congregation. One must be in good standing in the congregation to use the platform. Comments brothers make from the platform carry great weight. Here the training and role-playing for door-to-door witnessing also takes place; women are allowed to participate in role-playing activities.

Presiding Overseer. The elder who is the chairman of the elder body in a congregation.

Prophet (The). The Watchtower organization.

Public reprimand. A situation in which a person has not yet been disfellowshiped but is being watched, and close fellowship with that individual is discouraged.

Publisher. A faithful part-time (average 17 hours per month) Witness missionary who under the direction of WBTS shares Watchtower literature and doctrine with non-Witnesses door-to-door, participates in the Witness preaching activity, attends several weekly meetings and services, and keeps records of missionary activities. *See also* Kingdom publishers.

Ransom. Christ's death, which, although not necessary, purchased an opportunity for every human creature to be saved if he or she will believe and obey. The doctrine of the "ransom" formally resembles orthodoxy, but Christ is not regarded as an eternal being of infinite worth or as the One who endured God's wrath in the sinner's stead.

Reinstatement. The Elder Body's reacceptance into the organization of a person who had been disfellowshiped or who had disassociated himself or herself.

Remnant. Collective name given to those living who claim to be part of the Anointed Class of 144,000 who will inherit heavenly life when they die.

Resurrection. Restoration to life of the nonexistent dead.

Resurrection of Christ. Witnesses believe that Christ became nonexistent when he died and that he was raised three days later as a "spirit"—an angel. They deny his bodily resurrection. Along with their teaching that Christ returned invisibly in 1914, Witnesses believe that he raised dead Christians to "spirit life" shortly thereafter and that the rest of the human dead will be raised bodily during the thousand-year reign of God's kingdom.

Russell, Charles Taze. Founder and first president of the Jehovah's Witness movement, he was born in 1852 and died in 1916. He was known for his prolific writing and powerful ego.

Russellite. A follower of Charles Taze Russell, founder of the Jehovah's Witnesses.

Rutherford, Joseph Franklin. Born in 1869, "Judge" Rutherford became the second president of the WBTS in 1917. He is responsible for much of the present-day organization of the Society. He died in 1942.

Salvation. Although paying lip service to salvation through faith in Christ, Witnesses believe salvation is impossible apart from obedience to the

Watchtower Society and participation in its works program. Even individual Witnesses who are not sufficiently zealous may not survive Armageddon, and those who make their way into paradise on earth must maintain good works throughout Christ's thousand-year reign before they can be sealed for life. Witnesses are not sure when they have done enough or if they can be assured of salvation. Christians have this certainty through Christ—sharing this is the key in reaching Jehovah's Witnesses in love.

Satan. Spirit creature who is the adversary of God, believed to be misleading the entire inhabited earth, particularly since 1914 when he was cast out of heaven. *See also* Lucifer.

Servant. A brother who has been assigned responsibility in the congregation as an elder or ministerial servant.

Service meeting. An hour-long (later changed to 45 minutes) weekly meeting held at the Kingdom Hall, focused primarily on teaching and recruiting methods to be used when preaching to outsiders. *See also* Theocratic Ministry School.

Service report. Monthly report every active Witness is required to turn in, indicating how many hours he or she has spent in the preaching work, how many magazines and books were placed with non-Witnesses, how many follow-up visits were made, and how many Bible studies the Witness conducted that month.

Sheep. A Jehovah's Witness or a person interested in the message of the Witnesses.

Sheol. *See* Hades.

Shunning. *See* Disassociation, Disfellowshiping, Expelling.

Sister. A baptized female Jehovah's Witness.

Society (The). The Watchtower Bible and Tract Society, consisting of the Governing Body and the various committees they have selected to assist them; WBTS leaders who are supposedly directed by God. The Society's headquarters are in New York City. Responsible for overseeing publication of all Witness literature. All Witnesses must submit completely to the Society's authority. *See also* Organization.

Soul. A living creature; a human being does not possess a soul separate and distinct from the body.

Soul-sleep. The state of unconsciousness into which the soul of the Christian passes at death, until the return of Christ. Unbelievers are annihilated, but believers will be recreated at Christ's return.

Special pioneers. Full-time, salaried employees of the Watchtower Society, who spend at least 150 hours per month in religious service.

Spiritual food. Doctrines, scriptural interpretations, literature, Kingdom Hall meetings, assemblies, and conventions established by the Watchtower Society.

Stake. *See* Cross, Impalement.

Students Association Kingdom Hall. This local meeting house is never pretentious and is usually limited to a seating capacity of two hundred. Meetings are presided over by an overseer and five assistants. *See also* Kingdom Hall.

Stumble. To cause a person to leave the organization because of poor conduct by a Witness.

Temple. Jehovah's Witnesses are the "temple" of Christ, to which he returned in 1918.

Territory. The geographical area assigned to each congregation to cover in the preaching work. Attending a congregation outside one's territory is viewed as spiritual weakness, unless the organization instructs one to do so for a specific purpose.

Theocracy. Direct rule by God. Jehovah's Witnesses do not have a democratic organization. They submit to the control of a few leaders and believe that the entire organization is under the direct rule of Jehovah.

Theocratic. Word describing a person or event adhering to all the Society's rules. *See also* Untheocratic.

Theocratic Ministry School. Meeting that is held for about an hour each week at the Kingdom Hall. This school teaches Witnesses communication and speaking skills through giving short talks to the congregation, to equip them for door-to-door witnessing. All Witnesses are expected to participate. The service meeting and Theocratic Ministry School are usually held back to back for about a two-hour meeting. *See also* Service meeting.

This System of Things. The world as we presently know it.

Torture Stake. *See* Cross, Impalement.

Trinity. According to WBTS, a false, unbiblical doctrine. Jehovah's Witnesses reject the Trinity. Jehovah God is alone in authority and has no equal. Jesus is a being created by Jehovah. The Holy Spirit is not a person but an active force of God.

Truth. The teachings of the Watchtower Society at any given time, believed to be the only and absolute reality from God.

Untheocratic. Word describing a person or an event that does not adhere to all of the Society's rules. *See also* Theocratic.

Watch Tower. The official periodical publication of the Witnesses. *See also* Watchtower.

Watchtower Bible and Tract Society (WBTS) The official legal organization in use by Jehovah's Witnesses. Headquartered in New York City, WBTS prepares publications for the organization.

Watchtower. (Full title: *The Watchtower Announcing Jehovah's Kingdom.*) First published in 1879 and now a semimonthly magazine, *Watchtower* is the official theological publication of WBTS. The stated purpose of this semimonthly magazine is to exalt Jehovah God and keep watch on world events as they fulfill biblical prophecy. The unsigned articles present WBTS positions on biblical doctrines. WBTS issues an official compilation of all materials published since 1930.

Watchtower **study.** Weekly meeting of Jehovah's Witnesses, with question-and-answer study of *Watchtower* feature articles, held in every Kingdom Hall, usually on Sunday.

WBTS. *See* Watchtower Bible and Tract Society.

Wine and strong drink. Alcoholic drinks are regarded as gifts from Jehovah but must be used in moderation (Psalm 104:14,15). Drunkenness is condemned in the Bible. Habitual drunkenness is cause for expulsion from the congregation (1 Corinthians 5:11-13). There are also times one should not drink wine or liquor (Leviticus 10:8-11; Romans 14:21).

World. Life outside of the organization.

Worldly. Term used to describe people who are not Jehovah's Witnesses or to describe Witnesses who have untheocratic attitudes.

Year. In prophecy, it is often used in a special sense as the equivalent of 360 days (12 months of 30 days each). It is also called a time and sometimes a day.

Yearbook of Jehovah's Witnesses. Published annually by the Society, it reports worldwide activities, statistics, and service of faithful members. Daily Bible readings and commentary are also included.

The vocabulary was compiled and adapted from various sources, most of which are in the bibliography.

Bibliography

Jehovah's Witness Sources

Books

Aid to Bible Understanding. Brooklyn: Watch Tower Bible and Tract Society, 1971.

"Babylon the Great Has Fallen!" God's Kingdom Rules! Brooklyn: Watch Tower Bible and Tract Society, 1963.

Cole, Marley. *Triumphant Kingdom.* New York: Criterion Books, 1957.

From Paradise Lost to Paradise Regained. Brooklyn: Watch Tower Bible and Tract Society, 1958.

Is This Life All There Is? Brooklyn: Watch Tower Bible and Tract Society, 1974.

Jehovah's Witnesses: Proclaimers of God's Kingdom. Brooklyn: Watch Tower Bible and Tract Society, 1993.

"Let God Be True." Brooklyn: Watch Tower Bible and Tract Society, 1946.

"Make Sure of All Things Hold Fast to What Is Fine." Brooklyn: Watch Tower Bible and Tract Society, 1965.

"The Nations Shall Know That I Am Jehovah"—How? Brooklyn: Watch Tower Bible and Tract Society, 1971.

New World Translation of the Holy Scriptures. Brooklyn: Watch Tower Bible and Tract Society, 1961.

New World Translation of the Holy Scriptures. Brooklyn: Watch Tower Bible and Tract Society, revised 1984.

Qualified to Be Ministers. Brooklyn: Watch Tower Bible and Tract Society, 1955.

Reasoning From the Scriptures. Brooklyn: Watch Tower Bible and Tract Society, 1989.

Sing Praises to Jehovah. Brooklyn: Watch Tower Bible and Tract Society, 1984.

"The Truth Shall Make You Free." Brooklyn: Watch Tower Bible and Tract Society, 1943.

The Truth That Leads to Eternal Life. Brooklyn: Watch Tower Bible and Tract Society, 1968.

You Can Live Forever in Paradise on Earth. Brooklyn: Watch Tower Bible and Tract Society, 1989.

You May Survive Armageddon Into God's New World. Brooklyn: Watch Tower Bible and Tract Society, 1955.

"Your Will Be Done on Earth." Brooklyn: Watch Tower Bible and Tract Society, 1958.

Periodicals

Awake! Monthly magazine. Brooklyn: Watch Tower Bible and Tract Society.

Watchtower. Semimonthly magazine. Brooklyn: Watch Tower Bible and Tract Society.

Tracts

"All Suffering Soon to End!" Brooklyn: Watch Tower Bible and Tract Society, 2005.

"Comfort for the Depressed." Brooklyn: Watch Tower Bible and Tract Society, 2000.

"Do You Have an Immortal Spirit?" Brooklyn: Watch Tower Bible and Tract Society, 2001.

"Enjoy Family Life." Brooklyn: Watch Tower Bible and Tract Society, 1998.

"Hellfire: Is It Part of Divine Justice?" Brooklyn: Watch Tower Bible and Tract Society, 1995.

"Jehovah's Witnesses: What Do They Believe?" Brooklyn: Watch Tower Bible and Tract Society, 1992.

"Jehovah Who Is He?" Brooklyn: Watch Tower Bible and Tract Society, 1998.

"Life in a Peaceful New World." Brooklyn: Watch Tower Bible and Tract Society, 1994.

"What Do Jehovah's Witnesses Believe?" Brooklyn: Watch Tower Bible and Tract Society, 1987.

"What Hope for Dead Loved Ones?" Brooklyn: Watch Tower Bible and Tract Society, 1987.

"Who Are Jehovah's Witnesses." Brooklyn: Watch Tower Bible and Tract Society, 1995.

"Who Really Rules the World?" Brooklyn: Watch Tower Bible and Tract Society, 1992.

"Why You Can Trust the Bible." Brooklyn: Watch Tower Bible and Tract Society, 1987.

"Will This World Survive?" Brooklyn: Watch Tower Bible and Tract Society, 2005.

"Would You Like to Know More About the Bible?" Brooklyn: Watch Tower Bible and Tract Society, 2001.

Web site

Watchtower: Official Web Site of Jehovah's Witnesses. http://www.watchtower.org/

In addition to material produced by the Watch Tower Bible and Tract Society of Pennsylvania (the official designation still used in Jehovah's Witness publications), a great amount of the Society's material has been reproduced (often photographically) in non-Witness publications, such as Duane Magnani's *Watchtower Files,* Robert Morey's *How to Answer a Jehovah's Witness,* and the works of David Reed.

Non-Jehovah's Witness Sources

Books

Botting, Heather, and Gary Botting. *The Orwellian World of Jehovah's Witnesses.* Toronto: University of Toronto Press, 1984.

Bowman, Robert M., Jr. *Understanding Jehovah's Witnesses: Why They Read the Bible the Way They Do.* Grand Rapids: Baker, 1991.

———. *Why You Should Believe in the Trinity: An Answer to Jehovah's Witnesses.* Grand Rapids: Baker, 1989.

Cares, Mark J. *Speaking the Truth in Love to Mormons.* WELS Outreach Resources, 1998.

Clark, Elmer T. *Small Sects in America.* Nashville: Abingdon, 1965.

Dencher, Ted. *Why I Left Jehovah's Witnesses.* Fort Washington, PA: Christian Literature Crusade, 1980.

Ellwood, Robert S., and Barbara A. McGraw. *Many People, Many Faiths: Women and Men in the World Religions.* Eighth edition. Upper Saddle River, NJ: Pearson Prentice Hall, 2005.

Enroth, Ronald, ed. *A Guide to New Religious Movements.* Downers Grove, IL: InterVarsity, 2005.

Franz, Raymond. *Crisis of Conscience.* Atlanta: Commentary Press, 1983.

Gerstner, John H. *The Teachings of the Jehovah's Witnesses.* Grand Rapids: Baker, 1960.

Harrison, Barbara Grizzuti. *Visions of Glory: A History and a Memory of Jehovah's Witnesses.* New York: Simon and Schuster, 1978.

Hewitt, Joe. *I Was Raised a Jehovah's Witness: The True Story of a Former J. W.* Denver: Accent, 1979.

Hoekema, Anthony A. *The Four Major Cults: Christian Science, Jehovah's Witnesses, Mormonism, Seventh-day Adventism.* Grand Rapids: Eerdmans, 1963.

Hoerber, Robert G., ed. *Concordia Self-Study Bible: New International Version.* St. Louis: Concordia, 1984.

Kauffeld, Shawn E. *A House of Sand.* Spring Valley, WI: Books of the Way, 1999.

Kern, Herbert. *How to Respond to the Jehovah's Witnesses.* Revised edition. St. Louis: Concordia, 1995.

Lange, Lyle W. *God So Loved the World: A Study of Christian Doctrine.* Milwaukee: Northwestern, 2005.

Luther, Martin. *What Luther Says: An Anthology.* Three volumes. Complied by Ewald M. Plass. St. Louis: Concordia, 1959.

Magnani, Duane. *The Watchtower Files: Dialogue with a Jehovah's Witness.* Minneapolis: Bethany, 1983, 1985.

Martin, Walter. *The Kingdom of the Cults.* Minneapolis: Bethany, 1985.

Mather, George A., and Larry A. Nichols. *Dictionary of Cults, Sects, Religions and the Occult.* Grand Rapids: Zondervan, 1993.

Mayer, F. E. *Jehovah's Witnesses.* St. Louis: Concordia, 1957.

Morey, Robert A. *How to Answer a Jehovah's Witness: How to Successfully Take the Initiative When They Come to Your Door.* Minneapolis: Bethany, 1980.

Myers, Allen C., ed. *The Eerdmans Bible Dictionary.* Grand Rapids: Eerdmans, 1987.

Noll, Mark, et al., eds. *Eerdmans' Handbook to Christianity in America.* Grand Rapids: Eerdmans, 1983.

Penton, M. James. *Apocalypse Delayed: The Story of Jehovah's Witnesses.* Toronto: University of Toronto Press, 1985.

Reed, David A. *Index of Watchtower Errors*. Grand Rapids: Baker, 1990.

———. *Jehovah's Witnesses Answered Verse by Verse*. Grand Rapids: Baker, 1986.

Rhodes, Ron. *Reasoning From the Scriptures With the Jehovah's Witnesses*. Eugene, OR: Harvest House, 1993.

Schaff, Philip. *History of the Christian Church,* Vol. 3. *Nicene and Post-Nicene Christianity*. Grand Rapids: Eerdmans, 1910.

Schnell, William J. *How to Witness to Jehovah's Witnesses*. Grand Rapids: Baker, 1975.

———. *Thirty Years a Watchtower Slave: The Confessions of a Converted Jehovah's Witness*. Grand Rapids: Baker, 1971.

Stevenson, William C. *The Inside Story of Jehovah's Witnesses*. New York: Hart, 1968.

Trombley, Charles. *Kicked Out of the Kingdom*. Monroeville, PA: Whitaker House, 1974.

Van Baalen, Jan Karel. *The Chaos of the Cults: A Study in Present-Day Isms*. Grand Rapids: Eerdmans, 1972.

Wilson, Diane. *Awakening of a Jehovah's Witness: Escape From the Watchtower Society*. Amherst, NY: Prometheus, 2002.

Wisconsin Evangelical Lutheran Synod, authorized by. *Christian Worship: A Lutheran Hymnal*. Milwaukee: Northwestern, 1993.

Articles

Bergman, Jerry. "Paradise Postponed . . . and Postponed: Why Jehovah's Witnesses Have a High Mental Illness Level." *Christian Research Journal*. Vol. 19, No. 1 (Summer 1996): 36-41.

Bodine, Marian. "A Beginner's Guide to Witnessing to Jehovah's Witnesses." *Christian Research Newsletter*. Vol. 9, No. 1 (Winter/Spring 1996): 14-5.

Bowman, Robert M., Jr. "Is Jesus a True or a False God?" *Christian Research Journal*. Vol. 13, No. 1 (Winter/Spring 1990): 7.

———. "Jehovah's Witnesses and Luke 23:43." *Christian Research Journal*. Vol. 12, No. 1 (Summer 1989): 23.

———. "Jehovah's Witnesses and the Divine Name." *Christian Research Journal*. Vol. 12, No. 2 (Fall 1989): 21-3.

———. "The New World Translation on Trial." *Christian Research Journal*. Vol. 11, No. 2 (Fall 1989): 28.

———. "Watchtower Authority and the Bible." *Christian Research Journal*. Vol. 11, No. 2 (Fall 1988): 19.

———. "The Whitewashing of the Watchtower: How Jehovah's Witnesses Are Defending Their Faith." *Forward* (Spring-Summer) 1986: 9-14.

Bowman, Robert M., Jr., and Brian A. Onken. "Was Jesus Raised as a Spirit Creature? Dialoguing With Jehovah's Witnesses on 1 Corinthians 15:44-50." *Christian Research Journal*. Vol. 10, No. 1 (Summer 1987): 7.

Ehlke, Roland Cap. "350 Years Without Christmas." *Northwestern Lutheran* (December 1984): 340-1.

Finnerty, Robert U. "Faith of Our Fathers: Were the Early Christians Jehovah's Witnesses?" *Christian Research Journal*. Vol. 18, No. 3-4 (Winter/Spring 1996): 29-35, 37-43.

Goeldelman, M. Kurt. "Watchtower Announces Organization Changes." *Personal Freedom Outreach*. 2001. http://www.pfo.org/wtchange.htm.

Gruss, Edmond C. "Faithful and Wise Servant: Examining the Watch Tower's 1919 Appointment." *Christian Research Journal*. Vol. 26, No. 3 (2003): 22-31.

Gruss, Edmond C, and Jay Hess. "Is It Proper to Worship Jesus? Examining a Jehovah's Witness Doctrine." *Christian Research Journal*. Vol. 23, No. 4 (2001): 22-5, 42-6.

Gruss, Edmond C., and Leonard Chretien. "Beth-Sarim: A Monument to a False Prophet and False Prophecy." *Christian Research Journal*. Vol. 20, No. 1 (Summer 1997): 22-9.

———. "Beth-Shan and the Return of the 'Princes': The Untold Story." *Christian Research Journal*. Vol. 20, No. 2 (November/December 1997): 35-41.

Hailson, Donna F. G. "A Summary Critique: *Jehovah's Witnesses Defended*." *Christian Research Journal*. Vol. 21, No. 2 (1998): 47-9.

Martin, Walter. "Jehovah's Witnesses and the Doctrine of Death." *Christian Research Newsletter*. Vol. 5, No. 3 (1994).

Metzger, Bruce M. "The Jehovah's Witnesses and Jesus Christ: A Biblical and Theological Appraisal." *Theology Today* (April 1953): 65-84.

"Nathan Knorr's Armageddon: The Golden Years of Nathan H. Knorr." http://www.exjws.net/museum/knorr.htm.

Passantino, Gretchen. "Are Jehovah's Witnesses Giving Up on Their Blood Transfusion Ban." *Christian Research Journal*. Vol. 23, No. 2 (2000): 6-7.

———. "Jehovah's Witnesses Change Corporate Profile." *Christian Research Journal*. Vol. 23, No. 3 (2001): 6-9.

———. "Jehovah's Witnesses Child Abuse Cover-Up Alleged." *Christian Research Journal*. Vol. 25, No. 2 (2002): 53.

Passantino, Robert, and Gretchen Passantino. "Help for Your Loved One in a Cult." *Christian Research Journal*. Vol. 20, No. 4 (April/June 1998): 8, 46.

Ramer, Rachel. "Examining Translations With Jehovah's Witnesses." *Christian Research Journal.* Vol. 22, No. 3 (2000): 10-1.

Reed, David A. "Discussing Deity With Jehovah's Witnesses." *Christian Research Journal.* Vol. 11, No. 1 (Summer 1988): 7.

———. "Watchtower Issues New Instructions on Blood." *Christian Research Journal.* Vol. 15, No. 1 (Winter 1992): 5.

———. "Whither the Watchtower?: An Unfolding Crisis for Jehovah's Witnesses." Summer 1993. Christian Research Institute Statement DJ550. http://www.equip.org/free/DJ550.htm.

Rhodes, Ron. "Crucifixion by Cross." http://www.soulright.com/cross_rhodes.html.

Rush, Robert, and Debbie Rush. "Jehovah's Witnesses, A Name I Was Barely Acquainted With." *Christian Research Newsletter.* Vol. 11, No. 3 (1988).

White, James. "Effectively Sharing the Deity of Christ With Jehovah's Witnesses." *Christian Research Journal.* Vol. 20, No. 2 (November/December 1997): 8, 43.

———. "What Really Happened at the Council of Nicea?" *Christian Research Journal.* Vol. 20, No. 1 (Spring 1997): 28-34.

Web sites and e-mails

Answers.com. "Jehovah's Witnesses." http://www.answers.com/topic/jehovah-s-witnesses#wp-_note-54.

Challenging the Cults: "History of Jehovah's Witnesses." http://www.truthnet.org/Christianity/Cults/Jehovahwitness5/

Christian Apologetics and Research Ministry. Web site. http://www.carm.org/index.html.

Luke, Donald. E-mails and discussions with the author. Summer 2006.

Mueller, Amy. E-mails and discussions with the author. Summer 2006.

Wikipedia, The Free Encyclopedia. "Jehovah's Witnesses." http://en.wikipedia.org/wiki/Jehovah%27s_Witnesses.

Subject Index

Scripture Index

10:2-4—3
10:17—183
13:1-7—182
14:5,6—140
14:8,9—61
14:21—209
15:30—70

1 Corinthians
1:2—81
2:10,11—70
2:11—81
5:11-13—209
6:9,10—121
8:5,6—60
8:6—63,81
10:4—168,179
11:3—82
12:3—183
12:11—70
13:1,13—160
15:28—82
16:13—175

2 Corinthians
4:4—77
5:14—167
5:14,15—181
5:18,19—181

Galatians
1:1—104
3:1-3—122,123
3:26—76
4:4—101
5:1—132
6:14—136

Ephesians
1:23—68
2:1,2—125
2:8,9—120,162

4:10—68
4:14,15—1
4:30—70
6—101

Philippians
2:6—76
2:6-11—83
2:9-11—84
2:10,11—179
2:21—86

Colossians
1:15—85
1:15,16—84
1:16,17—86
1:19—87
2:9—87
2:16—141

1 Thessalonians
4:16—77
5:1,2—108

2 Thessalonians
2:7,8—12

1 Timothy
1:1—179
2:5—83
6:10—141
6:15—179

2 Timothy
1:7—158
3:1—151
3:16—56
4:6—68

Titus
2:14—121
3:5—122